Simulation Modelling Practice and Theory

Edited by Evon Abu-Taieh
and Asim Abdel El Sheikh Ahmed

Published in London, United Kingdom

IntechOpen

Supporting open minds since 2005

Simulation Modelling Practice and Theory
http://dx.doi.org/10.5772/intechopen.77500
Edited by Evon Abu-Taieh and Asim Abdel El Sheikh Ahmed

Contributors
Guolei Tang, Emilio Jimenez, Juan Ignacio Latorre-Biel, Jan Trąbka, Evon M.O. Abu-Taieh

Notice
Statements and opinions expressed in the chapters are these of the individual contributors and not
necessarily those of the editors or publisher. No responsibility is accepted for the accuracy of
information contained in the published chapters. The publisher assumes no responsibility for any
damage or injury to persons or property arising out of the use of any materials, instructions, methods
or ideas contained in the book.

First published in London, United Kingdom, 2019 by IntechOpen
IntechOpen is the global imprint of INTECHOPEN LIMITED, registered in England and Wales,
registration number: 11086078, The Shard, 25th floor, 32 London Bridge Street
London, SE19SG – United Kingdom
Printed in Croatia

British Library Cataloguing-in-Publication Data
A catalogue record for this book is available from the British Library

Additional hard copies can be obtained from orders@intechopen.com

Simulation Modelling Practice and Theory
Edited by Evon Abu-Taieh and Asim Abdel El Sheikh Ahmed
p. cm.
Print ISBN 978-1-78985-363-6
Online ISBN 978-1-78985-364-3

We are IntechOpen,
the world's leading publisher of
Open Access books
Built by scientists, for scientists

4,000+
Open access books available

116,000+
International authors and editors

120M+
Downloads

Our authors are among the

151
Countries delivered to

Top 1%
most cited scientists

12.2%
Contributors from top 500 universities

Interested in publishing with us?
Contact book.department@intechopen.com

Numbers displayed above are based on latest data collected.
For more information visit www.intechopen.com

Meet the editors

Evon Abu-Taieh (associate professor) has more than 29 years of experience in the field of computer science. She has published more than 50 research and five scholarly books. She acquired her BSC and MSc in Computer Science from the USA and her PhD from Jordan in 2005. She is an editorial board member of a number of scientific journals. Abu-Taieh has held a number of posts: Dean of Computing Faculty (first women ever to hold such a post), Jordan University for three years; Chair of both CIS and BIT departments for two years, as well as general registrar; Commissioner for Air Transport for three years in civil aviation, Jordan, and Head of Computer Department for 10 years at the Ministry of Transport. Abu-Taieh worked as a reviewer at a number of renowned international conferences. Her research interests are simulation and modeling, AI, cyber security, knowledge management, project management, and software engineering.

Professor Asim Abdel Rahman El Sheikh Ahmed obtained a BSc (honors) (Statistics) from the University of Khartoum (Sudan), and an MSc (Operational Research) and PhD (Computer Simulation) from the University of London (UK). He has worked for the University of Khartoum, Philadelphia University (Jordan), the Arab Academy for Banking, Financial Sciences (Jordan), and Al-Ahliyya Amman University (Jordan). Professor El Sheikh is currently the research manager at the Onyx Link Foundation (Wales, UK). He has a vast record in the areas of research, training, and consultancy. His research interests include computer simulation and software engineering.

Contents

Preface

Simulation and modeling is an approach used when everything fails. Simulation and modeling applications range from nuclear reactions to transport systems. Hence, there are two types of simulation approaches: discrete simulation approaches and continuous simulation approaches. The process interaction approach, event scheduling approach, activity scanning approach, and three-phase approach all belong to the first family. In the process interaction approach the computer program emulates the flow of an object through the system. The transaction flow approach is a simpler version of the process interaction approach. The event scheduling approach advances time to the moment when something happens next. The third approach, the activity scanning approach, is based on two phases: the first phase executes after a fixed amount of time, the second phase executes after the satisfaction of some condition. The fourth approach is the three-phase approach, and as the name is suggests it has three phases: A, B, and C.

To handle concurrent discrete event dynamic systems, Petri nets were developed by Carl Adam at the beginning of the 1960s as a theory for discrete parallel systems. Such an idea is reflected in the chapter "Petri net models optimized for simulation."

Simulation and modeling needs imagination and innovations to be developed from scratch. Yet, simulation is needed, hence the question: why do we simulate? Simulation allows experimentation rather than direct, costly, time-consuming experimentation. Simulation allows time control that the user can use to compress and expand the time element. Simulation experiments can be replicated to answer questions like: why did this happen? Simulation allows the user to explore possibilities. Simulation also allows the user to explore different possibilities while identifying constraints, predicting obstacles, and playing with what-if scenarios. Simulation is used to train pilots as well as medical professionals in new technology.

In this book three chapters tackle three simulation arenas:

The chapter titled "Petri net models optimized for simulation" presents two Petri net-based formalisms analyzed for profiting from their respective advantages of modeling, simulation, and decision-making support: a set of alternative Petri nets and a compound Petri net. These formalisms, as well as the transformation algorithms between them, are detailed and an illustrative example. Among the main advantages of these formalisms, their intuitive application for modeling discrete event systems in the process of being designed, as well as the compactness that may present the resulting model, in the case of a compound Petri net, which lead to efficient decision making, can be mentioned.

The chapter titled "Simulation modeling for ship traffic flow in entrance channels" uses process interaction-based simulation model for ship operation (PI-SMSO) using Java language to help designers to determine the dimensions of entrance channels. The PI-SMSO component simulates ships in and out of a one- or two-way traffic channel, or a one-way channel with a ships-passing anchorage, as well as ships discharging/loading at berths. Finally, we apply the PI-SMSO to a Chinese coal-import terminal to explore its possible bottlenecks by evaluating the performance of the entrance channel system, and determine the available improvement strategies according to the simulated port performance.

The chapter titled "The proposal for modeling methodology for Enterprise Content Management (ECM) systems—modeling tools selection" presents content management as one of the strategic directions of ICT development in modern enterprises. This trend is spurred by the increasing amount of data and explicit knowledge (that is, content) whose characteristic features are a lack of structure and multimediality. A dynamically growing market of ECM platforms, defined as the set of components and technologies used for managing content in any given area of the company, has emerged. Researchers focusing on ECM agree that the current aspect of content management is much more recognizable in business practice than in the theoretical and methodological ECM toolkit as a separate discipline of IS. This chapter presents the main elements of the author's methodology of modeling an enterprise that is preparing for ECM platform implementation. The working name of this methodology is Enterprise Content Management Modeling Method (ECM3). The modeling methodology is understood as a set of assumptions and perspectives of building the enterprise model, analytical tools to create it, and stages of the completion of the analytical process. The chapter presents the assumptions of methodology, selected analytical tools, as well as practical examples from actual ECM implementation.

Each chapter in this book explores one aspect of the simulation and modeling arena, reflecting the power of simulation and implementation of the concept, while using different approaches to solve a different problem—hence, reflecting multifaceted applications of simulation.

Evon Abu-Taieh
Faculty of Computer and Information Science,
Princess Nourah bint Abdulrahman University,
Riyadh, Saudi Arabia,

Asim Abdel El Sheikh Ahmed
The Onyx Link Foundation,
Newport, Wales, UK

Section 1

Introduction

Chapter 1

Introductory Chapter: Simulation and Modeling

Evon Abu-Taieh

1. Introduction

The influx of data in the world today needs analysis that no method can handle. Some reports estimated the influx of data to reach 163 zettabytes by 2025 and hence the need for simulation and modeling theory and practice. Simulation and modeling tools and techniques are of most importance in this day and age. While simulation carries the needed work, tools of visualizing the results help in decision-making process. Simulation ranges of simple queue to molecular dynamics include seismic reliability analysis, structural integrity assessment, games, reliability engineering, and system safety. This book will introduce simulation and modeling to practitioners, researchers, and novice users to the world of imagination.

Simulation and modeling programs are not like any other computer program. Section 1 can look at the amount of research being conducted in the scientific community, and the facts are reflected in Section 2. Section 3 shows the distinguishing factors of simulation. Section 4 presents classical simulation approaches and their handling of the time elements which is one of the distinguishing factors of simulation. Section 5 sheds light on the reasons why we simulation. Section 6 explains furthermore the different uses of simulation especially in training. Section 7 discusses the answer of proof of correctness or validation and verification question that is the second distinguishing feature of simulation.

2. Simulation in research

Simulation is a very important topic in the research community. According to the IEEE digital library in the year 2014, scientific journals and magazines published 9478 scientific research papers. In the year 2015, 10,371 scientific research papers were published, while in the year 2016, 11,133 scientific papers were published in journals and magazines. According to the same source in the year 2017, 12,206 scientific research papers were published. Hence, in the 4 years (2014–2017), 43,188 scientific research papers were published. The number indicates how rich the simulation topic is with undiscovered topics and many unsolved problems. Hence, the simulation topic is worth investigating.

3. Distinguishing features of simulation

There are four distinguishing characteristics that differentiate simulation from any computer program: time use simulation is an indexing variable, simulation

IntechOpen

objective is to achieve correctness, simulation is computational intensive, and there is no typical use of simulation [1]. As time is an indexing variable, the use of such variable can be discrete or continues. Such use of the time variable is reflected in the approaches and method of simulation.

The second feature is reflected in the discussion of validation and verification of the simulation program. The section lists ways of validation and verification. To achieve correctness is a major goal of any simulation program; furthermore, the proof of correctness is a challenge of simulation.

The third feature is also another challenge in simulation world. Simulation major feature is the time indexing variable, which is a challenge on its own. Another element that makes simulation computational intensive is animation. Animation in relation with time variable is very challenging to master in any simulation program.

The fourth feature is distinguishing of simulation; there is no typical use of simulation. Simulation is colored with its use. The uses of simulation range from transport systems to molecule interactions. Hence, simulation is colored from within its use.

4. Classical simulation approaches

Simulation and modeling is an approach used when everything fails. Simulation and modeling applications range from nuclear reactions to transport systems. Hence, there are two types of simulation approaches: discrete simulation approaches and continuous simulation approaches. Process interaction approach, event scheduling approach, activity scanning approach, stock and flow approach, and three-phase approach all belong to the first family. In process interaction approach, the computer program emulates the flow of an object through the system. Transaction flow approach is a simpler version of process interaction approach. Event scheduling approach advances time to the moment when something happens next. The third approach, activity scanning approach, is based on two phases: the first phase is the execution after a fixed amount of time, and the second phase is the execution after the satisfaction of some condition. The third approach is a three-phase approach; as the name is suggesting, it has three phases: A, B, and C. To better understand the simulation approaches, **Figure 1** reflects the flow charts of each of them.

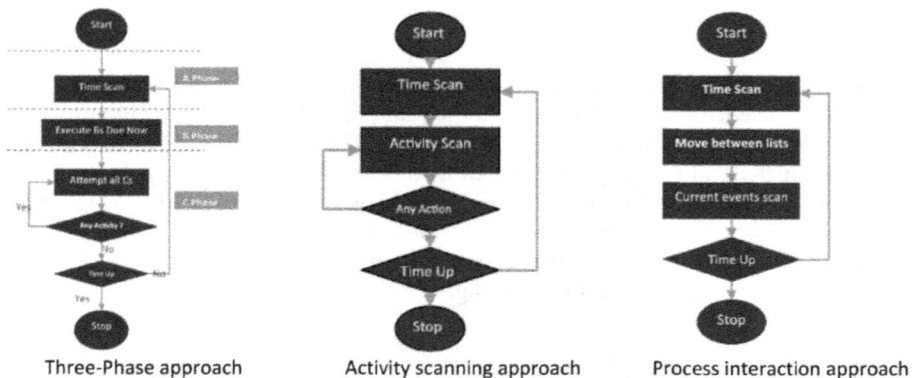

Three-Phase approach   Activity scanning approach   Process interaction approach

Figure 1.
Flow charts of the three classical simulation approaches [1].

To handle concurrent discrete event dynamic systems, Petri nets were developed by Carl Adam in the beginning of the 1960s, a theory for discrete parallel system. Such idea is reflected in the chapter "Petri Net Models Optimized for Simulation."

5. Why simulate?

Simulation and modeling needs imagination and innovations to be developed from scratch. Yet, simulation is needed and hence the question "why do we simulate?" Simulation allows experimentation rather than direct, costly, time-consuming experimentation. Simulation allows time control where the user can compress and expand time element. Simulation experiments can be replicated, so as to answer questions like "why did this happen?" Simulation allows the user to explore possibilities. Simulation allows the user to explore different possibilities while identifying constrains and predict obstacles. Playing with what-if scenarios, simulation is used to train pilots as well as medical professionals in the case of new technology.

6. Simulation uses in training

Simulation is used to train people in a number of arenas for many reasons: either the training situation is too dangerous to conduct or too delicate or too expensive. A study by Abu-Taieh and Abutayeh [2], they listed 12 areas where simulation is used for vocational training: to train pilots, many simulators are used. Rather than using the real plane to teach the pilot to fly, a simulator is used to train the pilot. Another use is to conduct chemical experiments by simulating the experiments. As such, the experimenter is in a safe environment while knowledge is transferred on handling chemical materials.

Another training arena is physics experiments. Simulators are used to conduct physics experiments. To teach things like motion, energy, power, sound, heat, electricity, magnets, circuits, light, and radiation, a simulator is used to teach their attributes and to visualize the experiments as seen in [3].

Mathematics, algebra, number theory, mathematical functions, trigonometry, data analysis, graphs, trees, networks, enumerative combinations, iteration, and recursion are hard topics to understand and visualize. Simulation is used as an explanatory tool and a visualizing method. Nelson [4] listed five reasons to use simulation in mathematics.

Simulation is used to study environmental and ecological systems. Since such arena is overwhelmed with variables that no mathematical formula can solve, simulation is used to study, visualize, understand, and explain environmental phenomena.

To study, understand, and explain cosmology and astrophysics, many computer-based simulators are used. Simulation in this case enhances the understanding of cosmology and astrophysics by visualization. Simulators are also used to train medical students in surgery training. Such concept is used to train novice surgeons to gain expertise and self-confidence before conducting the real surgery.

Simulators are also used in civil engineering, interior design, and architectural engineering designs. Since real-life experimentation is lengthy and expensive, simulators in such arena save time, money, and effort by delivering virtual product which can be altered rather than delivering real-life product. In Marshall et al. [5], healthcare delivery is discussed using simulation. Other uses of simulation are to design, understand, test, and visualize computers and communication networks as seen in [6, 7].

To learn financial planning and to model marketing simulation is used, namely, in Crystal Ball and Analytica, among others. Business modeling, risk analysis, cost/benefit analysis, and risk management are also taught using simulators. In military training, virtual reality (VR) and virtual augmented reality (VAR) are used. Simulators like mission rehearsal exercise (MRE).

A published research [8, 9] classified 56 simulation environment according to their 22 uses: air traffic control and space systems, supply chain management, business process reengineering and workflows, transportation systems, complex system design evaluation, aerospace, computer and communication networks, oil and gas, computer performance evaluation, construction, education and training, financial modeling, healthcare systems, parcels and parcel handling(queue), manufacturing systems, de-bottlenecking, military/combat systems, what-if scenarios, satellite and wireless communications systems, robotic and mechanical systems, service systems, and decision and risk analysis.

7. Validation, verification, and testing (VV&T) in simulation

This section is an answer to the second distinguishing feature of simulation. VV&T in simulation is the most important quest. There is no point in simulating the wrong model and no point in simulating the model incorrectly. Validation answers to the question "Are we building the right model?" Verification answers to the question "Are we building the product right?" These two questions have been raised back in 1995 when Balci [10] published a research paper listing 15 simulation VV&T principles, as follows:

1. *V&V must be conducted throughout the entire M&S life cycle.*

2. *The outcome of VV&A should not be considered as a binary variable where the model or simulation is absolutely correct or absolutely incorrect.*

3. *A simulation model is built with respect to the M&S objectives, and its credibility is judged with respect to those objectives.*

4. *V&V requires independence to prevent developer's bias.*

5. *VV&A is difficult and requires creativity and insight.*

6. *Credibility can be claimed only for the prescribed conditions for which the model or simulation is verified, validated, and accredited.*

7. *Complete simulation model testing is not possible.*

8. *VV&A must be planned and documented.*

9. *Type I, II, and III errors must be prevented.*

10. *Errors should be detected as early as possible in the M&S life cycle.*

11. *Multiple response problem must be recognized and resolved properly.*

12. *Successfully testing each submodel (module) does not imply overall model credibility.*

13. *Double validation problem must be recognized and resolved properly.*

14. *Simulation model validity does not guarantee the credibility and acceptability of simulation results.*

15. *A well-formulated problem is essential to the acceptability and accreditation of M&S results.*

In the same paper, Balci [10] divided the V&V techniques into two categories: V&V techniques for simulation models and V&V techniques for object-oriented simulation models. The V&V techniques for simulation models were further divided into four subcategories: informal, static, dynamic, and formal. V&V techniques for object-oriented simulation models were divided into three subcategories: conventional, adaptive, and specific. The informal subcategory included 8 V&V techniques, and the static subcategory included 19 techniques. The dynamic subcategory included 50 techniques. The formal subcategory included eight techniques. The adaptive subcategory included 15 techniques, while the specific subcategory included 31 techniques. In total, Balci listed more than 130 validation and verification techniques; as such, this only reflects the importance of validation and verification in simulation.

Some published work like [8, 9, 11, 12] discussed the validation and verification quest. The first two sources listed the different methods and tools for VV&T, and the third source developed a method from within the system development life cycle of simulation.

8. Conclusion

Playing the virtual world with time element is a joy and challenge. Hence, simulation to simulators is an open-ended question. This chapter showed the importance of simulation from academic and scientific point of view and then the distinguishing elements of simulation. Two distinguishing features stood out: time element and the correctness of the simulation program. Time element handling is reflected in Section 4. Correctness of the simulation program is discussed in Section 7. In the overall picture, simulation and modeling is like an addictive game that one can never get tired of.

Acknowledgements

I would like to acknowledge the efforts and support of Princess Nourah bint Abdulrahman University College of Computer and Information Sciences Dean Prof. Auhood Alfaries and the University of Jordan for their moral support and encouragement. Also, I would to acknowledge the Publisher **intechopen.com** and their people (Dajana Pemac, Author Service Manager, and Danijela Vladika), for the opportunity and their support, patience, and hard work.

Author details

Evon Abu-Taieh
Princess Nourah bint Abdulrahman University, Riyadh, Saudi Arabia

*Address all correspondence to: abutaieh@gmail.com

IntechOpen

References

[1] Abu-Taieh EM, Rahman El Sheikh AA, Abu-Tayeh JM, Abdallat HA. History of simulation. In: Khosrow-Pour M, editor. Encyclopedia of Information Science and Technology. 2nd ed. Hershey, PA: IGI Global; 2009. pp. 1769-1776. DOI: 10.4018/978-1-60566-026-4.ch278

[2] Abu-Taieh EM, Abutayeh JM. Simulation environments as vocational and training tools. In: Management Association, editor. Gaming and Simulations: Concepts, Methodologies, Tools and Applications. Hershey, PA: IGI Global; 2011. pp. 854-866. DOI: 10.4018/978-1-60960-195-9.ch317

[3] Maghsoodlou S, Afzali A. Simulation in classical nanomaterials: New development and achievements. Physics and Chemistry of Classical Materials: Applied Research and Concepts;2014. 235

[4] Nelson BL. Using simulation to teach probability. In: Proceeding of the 2002 Winter Simulation Conference; San Diego, CA, USA; 2002. p. 1815

[5] Marshall DA, Burgos-Liz L, IJzerman MJ, Crown W, Padula WV, Wong PK, et al. Selecting a dynamic simulation modeling method for health care delivery research—Part 2: Report of the ISPOR dynamic simulation modeling emerging good practices task force. Value in Health. 2015;18(2):147-160

[6] Al-Bahadili H, Issa G, Sabri A. Enhancing the performance of the DNDP algorithm. The International Journal of Wireless and Mobile Networks. 2011;3(2):113-124

[7] Al-Bahadili H. Enhancing the performance of adjusted probabilistic broadcast in MANETs. The Mediterranean Journal of Computers and Networks (MEDJCN). 2010;6(4):1992-1995

[8] Abu-Taieh EM, Rahman El Sheikh AA. Discrete event simulation process validation, verification, and testing. In: Dasso A, Funes A, editors. Verification, Validation and Testing in Software Engineering. Hershey, PA: IGI Global; 2007. pp. 177-212. DOI: 10.4018/978-1-59140-851-2.ch008

[9] Abu-Taieh E, El Sheikh A. Commercial simulation packages: A comparative study. International Journal of Simulation. 2007;8(2):66-76

[10] Balci O. Principles and techniques of simulation validation, verification, and testing. In: Alexopoulos C and Kang K, editors. Proceedings of the 27th conference on Winter simulation (WSC '95). Washington, DC, USA: IEEE Computer Society; 1995. pp. 147-154. DOI: 10.1145/224401.224456

[11] Abu-Taieh EM, Rahman El Sheikh AA. A road map for the validation, verification and testing of discrete event simulation. In: Khosrow-Pour M, editor. Encyclopedia of Information Science and Technology. 2nd ed. Hershey, PA: IGI Global; 2009. pp. 3306-3313. DOI: 10.4018/978-1-60566-026-4.ch526

[12] Abu-Taieh EM, Rahman El Sheikh AA, Abu Tayeh J. Relay race methodology (RRM): An enhanced life cycle for simulation system development. In: El Sheikh A et al., editors. Simulation and Modeling: Current Technologies and Applications. Hershey, PA: IGI Global; 2008. pp. 156-174. DOI: 10.4018/978-1-59904-198-8.ch005

Section 2

Simulation Use

Chapter 2

Simulation Modeling for Ship Traffic Flow in Entrance Channel

Tang Guolei and Qi Yue

Abstract

The design of coastal entrance channel is a complex challenge, considering the stochastic environment and time-consuming calculation works. Therefore, we implement a process-interaction-based simulation model for ship operation (PI-SMSO) using Java language to help the designers to determine the dimensions of entrance channels. The PI-SMSO component simulates ships in and out through a one- or two-way traffic channel, or a one-way channel with a ship-passing anchorage, and ships discharging/loading at berths. Finally, we apply the PI-SMSO to a Chinese coal-import terminal, to explore its possible bottlenecks by evaluating the performance of entrance channel system, and determine the available improvement strategies according to the simulated port performance. The case study proves that the proposed PI-SMSO effectively simulates the ship traffic flow in entrance channel and provides a decision support for evaluating entrance channel system.

Keywords: entrance channel, stochastics, process-interaction-based simulation, ship traffic flow

1. Introduction

A coastal entrance channel linking the berths of a port and the open sea is required to provide safe and convenient navigation for ships calling at ports. Recently, the rapid increase in the number and size of ships leads to further pressures on the entrance channels [1, 2]. For example, the Senate Appropriations Committee appropriated $33.5 million to deepen and widen the Houston Ship Channel, which deepened the channel from 12.2 to 13.7 m and widened it from 122 to 162 m [3–5]; Guangzhou Port will invest $484 million to expand its 66.6 km entrance channel into two-way traffic for container ships of 100,000 deadweight tons (DWT) [6]. Considering the high costs to expand entrance channels, a tool or model is needed to help the designers to evaluate the capacity of entrance channel and then to determine when to expand the channel and to select the dimensions of the expanded channel.

An entrance channel system can only be schematized as a complex system as it integrates with different ship types, the layout of water areas, and berths. In consideration of the stochastic characteristics of a port system, to explore the performance of integrated system, queuing theory is not applicable, and a simulation technique has to be used by simulating ship operations in and out of a port via entrance channels, e.g., a one- or two-way channel, especially a longer one-way channel with passing places [7, 8]. To simulate the complex port system, the "process description method" or "object-oriented method" is considered to be appropriate and efficient

[4, 5, 7]. Moreover, other important procedures, such as model verification and validation and simulation replication determination, should be conducted before productive simulation runs are started. It seems obvious that these procedures are impossibly time-consuming and complex for the designers. Therefore, we first developed a process-interaction-based simulation model for ship operation (PI-SMSO), which involves moving in and out of a port through entrance channels and handling cargoes at berths and automatically evaluates the performance of the stochastic port system. Finally, the effectiveness and applicability of the PI-SMSO are supported by a case study conducted at a coal terminal in China.

The remainder of this paper is organized as follows. First, the processes of ship operation in entrance channels are discussed for one- and two-way channels and one-way channels with ship-passing anchorage (SPAC). Next, this study implements a process-interaction-based simulation model for ship operation (PI-SMSO), and it classes for PI-SMSO. Then, the proposed PI-SMSO is applied to a Chinese coal-import terminal and used to evaluate entrance channel system and available improvement strategies. Finally, concluding remarks and future researches are presented.

2. Ship operation in entrance channels

2.1 Entrance channel types

The process of ship operation depends on the types of entrance channels, such as one- or two-way channels, and one-way channels with ship-passing anchorage (SPAC) [2, 4, 5, 9]. As shown in **Figure 1**, one-way channels only allow vessels to move in the same direction (**Figure 1(a)**), which is used for low ship traffic or when excavation of larger channel would be very expensive; two-way channels reduce one-way restrictions and allow inbound and outbound ships to pass each other (**Figure 1(b)**), which is considerable for improving navigation efficiency. However, expanding into a two-way channel costs highly by dredging/excavation especially for the very long channel. In some cases, a compromise is created by constructing SPAC along the longer one-way channel [7]. As illustrated in **Figure 1(c)**, the SPAC divides the channel into two parts (Channel *A* and *B*) and provides temporary moorings for lower-time-value ships (outbound ships in **Figure 1**) waiting until other vessels from opposite directions pass by. In this case, when outbound ships are traveling in Channel *B*, inbound ships can enter Channel *A* rather than waiting in the outside anchorage as shown in **Figure 1(a)**. In this way, ships traveling in opposite directions in a one-way channel can pass each other similar to a two-way channel.

2.2 Ship operation process

2.2.1 Ship traffic flow for one- and two-way channels

Figure 2 describes the flow of ship operations in one- and two-way entrance channels, which focuses on the activities conducted in the anchorage area, entrance channel, and at berths. As illustrated in **Figure 2(a)**, ship operation begins with the arrival of an inbound ship. This inbound ship may or may not wait in the anchorage area, depending on the state of weather, berth congestion, and channel navigability. As illustrated in **Figure 2(b)**, on days with good weather, the berth-assigned ship enters entrance channel in the following two cases: (1) for a one-way channel, no outbound ships are in the channel, and both the navigable depth and the distance between fore-and-aft inbound ships (if there are inbound ships in the channel, we call safety distance) satisfy the navigation requirement or

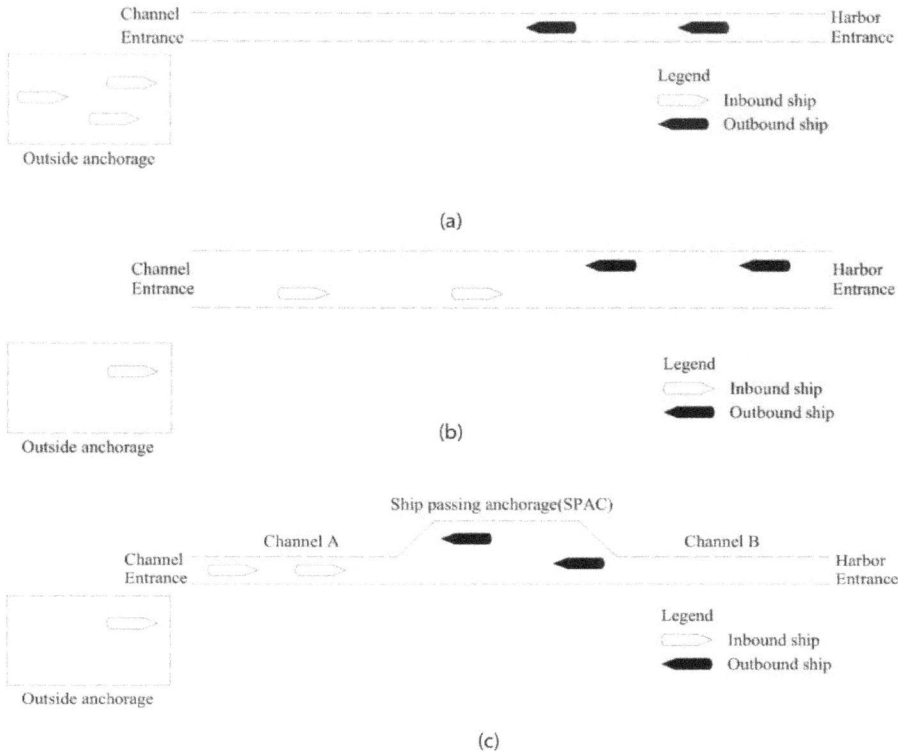

Figure 1.
A diagram of ship traffic flows in entrance channels including one- and two-way channels and a one-way channel with a SPAC. (a) Ship traffic flow for a one -way traffic channel. (b) Ship traffic flow for a two-way traffic channel. (c) Ship traffic flow for a one-way traffic channel with a SPAC.

(2) for a two-way channel, both the navigable depth and the safety distance satisfy the navigation requirement. Usually, this ship is guided by one or more tugboats to the assigned berth through entrance channel and then starts to unload (load) the cargoes onto (from) the quay after necessary preparation. Finally, once cargo unloading and loading is finished, outbound ship leaves berth, enters channel, and leaves port in the following three cases as illustrated in **Figure 2(c)** [7, 10]: (1) for a one-way channel, no inbound ships are in the channel, and both the navigable depth and safety distance satisfy the safety requirement or (2) for a two-way channel, both the navigable depth and safety distance satisfy the navigation requirement. If a port or entrance channel (or both) is closed due to adverse weather (i.e., strong winds, high waves, or heavy fog), we must know the number of days with adverse weather and how these heavy-weather days are usually distributed in a year.

2.2.2 Ship traffic flow for a one-way traffic channel with a SPAC

Figure 3(a) shows the overall logic of ship operations in a one-way channel with a SPAC. Setting a SPAC in a one-way channel changes the logic of checking channel availability in **Figure 2(a)**. The detail on changes is discussed in the following:

(1) **Figure 3(b)** illustrates the logic flowchart for checking channel availability for an inbound berth-assigned ship (CCA4IS). As shown in **Figure 3(b)**, on days with good weather, the berth-assigned inbound ship enters entrance channel in the

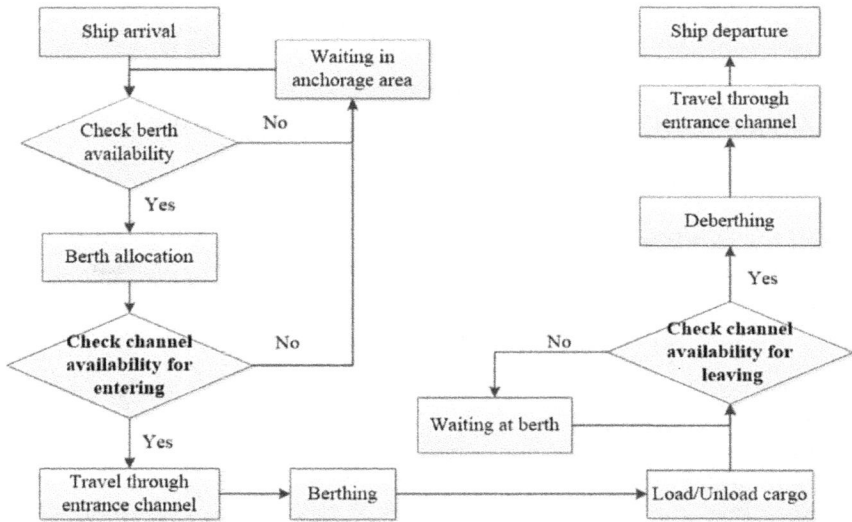

(a)

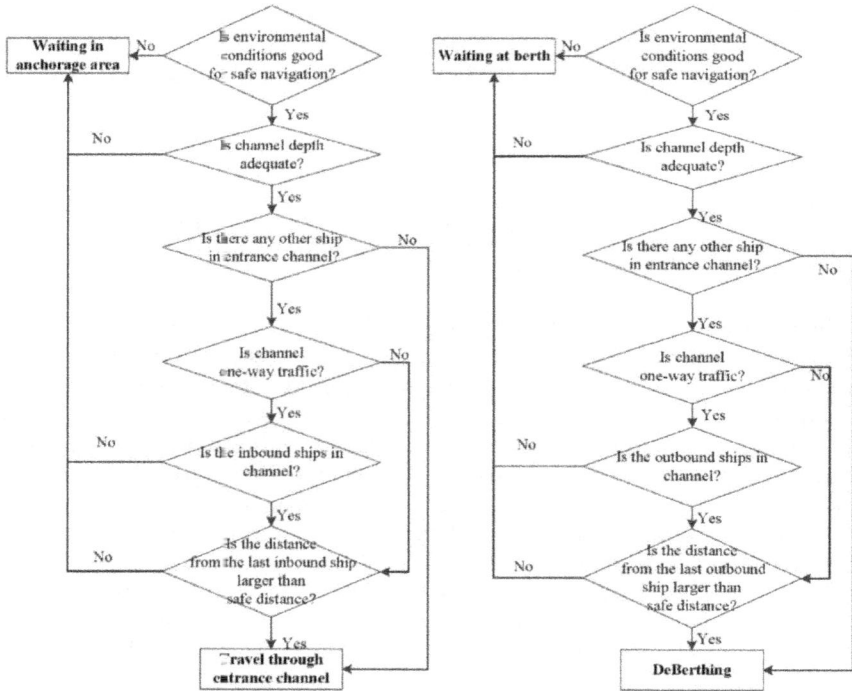

(b)

Figure 2.
The overall logic flowchart of ship operation simulation in one- and two-way traffic channels. (a) Overall logic flow. (b) Check channel availability for inbound ships. (c) Check channel availability for outbound ships.

following two cases: (1) if no outbound ships are traveling in both Channels *A* and *B*, both the navigable depth and safety distance satisfy the navigation requirement or (2) if only lower-priority outbound ships are traveling in Channel *B*, the SPAC

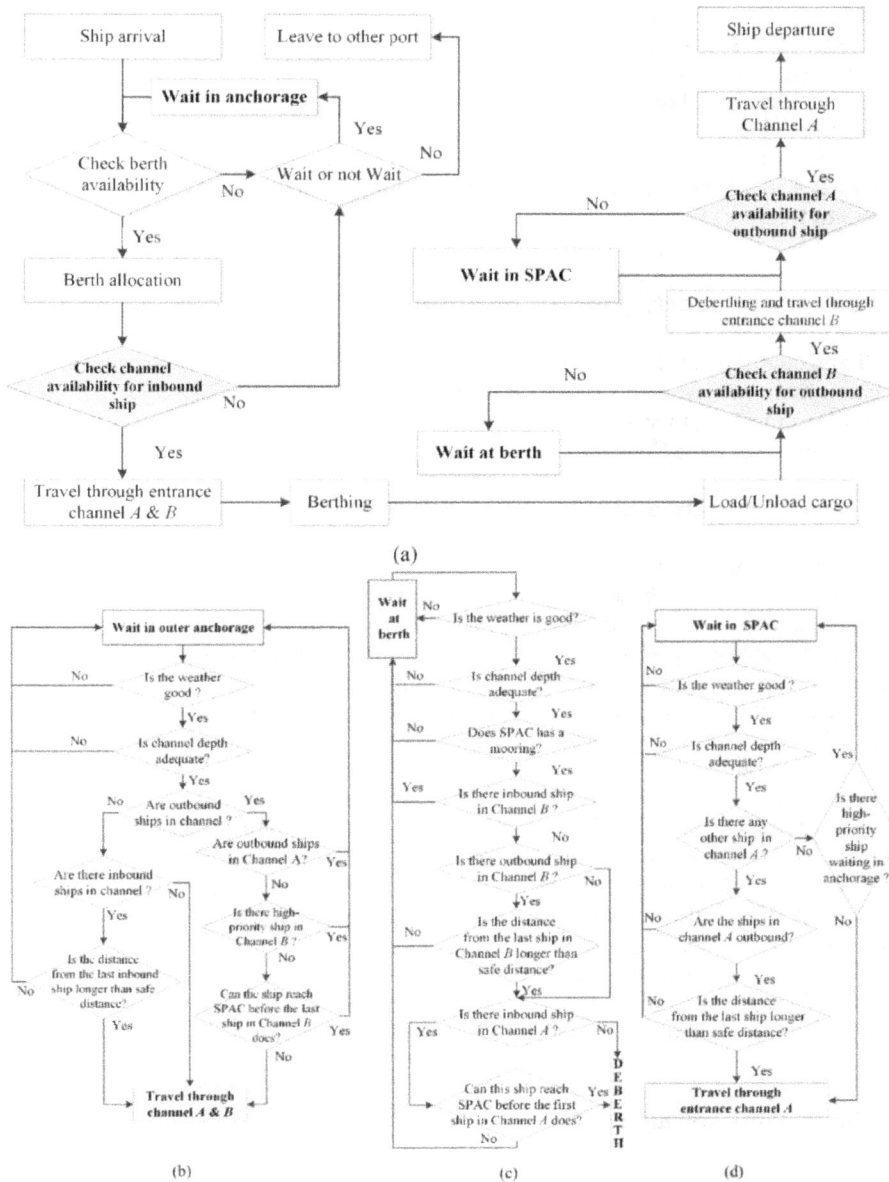

Figure 3.
The logic flowchart of ship operations for cargo-import ports with a SPAC (a) overall logic, (b) CCA4IS, (c) CCBA4OS, and (d) CCAA4OS.

can accommodate these outbound ships, and the last outbound ship in Channel *B* can reach the SPAC before this ship does.

(2) **Figure 3(c)** shows the logic of checking the availability of Channel *B* for an outbound ship at berth after finishing cargo unloading (CCBA4OS). As illustrated in **Figure 3(c)**, the ship deberths and enters entrance channel in the following two cases: (1) if no inbound ships are traveling in Channel *A*, the navigable depth and safety distance satisfy the safe navigation requirement or (2) if one or more inbound ships are traveling in Channel *A*, the SPAC has at least one idle mooring

position for this outbound ship, and this outbound ship can arrive at the SPAC before the first inbound ship in Channel *A*.

(3) **Figure 3(d)** checks the availability of Channel A for an outbound ship from the SPAC (CCAA4OS), and the ship leaves SPAC and enters Channel *A* in the following two cases: (1) no ships are traveling in Channel *A*, and no higher-priority ships are waiting in the outside anchorage or (2) if outbound ships are traveling in Channel *A*, both the navigable depth and the safety distance satisfy the safe navigation requirements.

3. Simulation modeling of ship operation

To evaluate the performance of the stochastic port system, we implement a process-interaction-based simulation model in Java™ [11], which simulates ship operations in one- or two-way channels, and a longer one-way channel with a SPAC according to the logic flowchart in Section 2.

3.1 Process-interaction-based simulation

There are basically three approaches that can be used for discrete event simulation: the event-based, the activity-based, and the process-interaction approach. Process-interaction simulation is a typical discrete event simulation paradigm. Since processes resemble objects in the real world, process-interaction simulation is often easy to understand, which is used in HLA (high-level architecture), DIS (distributed interactive simulation), and other object-oriented distributed simulations [12]. Therefore, we apply the process-interaction approach to the ship operation simulation model in this study.

The process-interaction worldview provides a way to represent a system's behavior from the active entities point of view according to the authors of SIMULA [13]. Thus, a system is modeled as a set of active entities in interaction, and the life cycle of each active entity consists of a sequence of events, activities, and delays. So in the ship operation simulation, a ship is an example of an active entity. Each ship performs the following sequence of activities: arrive at a port area, wait in the anchorage area, transit from anchorage area to berth, get cargo handled, leave the berth and enter the channel, and depart from port. Besides, the model also includes other components providing services for ships, such as anchorage area, entrance channel, and berth.

3.2 Simulation implementation

According to the process-interaction worldview, an active entity requires special mechanisms for interrupting, suspending, and resuming its execution at a later simulated time. Thus, Java programming language is suitable as it offers at least a SIMULA's coroutine-like mechanism. Therefore, we implement a process-interaction-based simulation model for ship operation (PI-SMSO) in Java programming language, and the implemented Java classes consist of foundational class library for process-interaction simulation (PIS library) and business class library for ship operation simulation (SOS library), as shown in **Figure 4**.

PIS library is a collection of public classes for process-interaction simulation, such as *Process*, *Entity*, *Queue*, and *Simulation* as shown in **Figure 4**. The *Process* class is the base class for a process-interaction simulation which extends *java.lang. Thread* and provides all of the necessary operations for the simulation system to control the simulation entities within it, and for them to interact with it and each

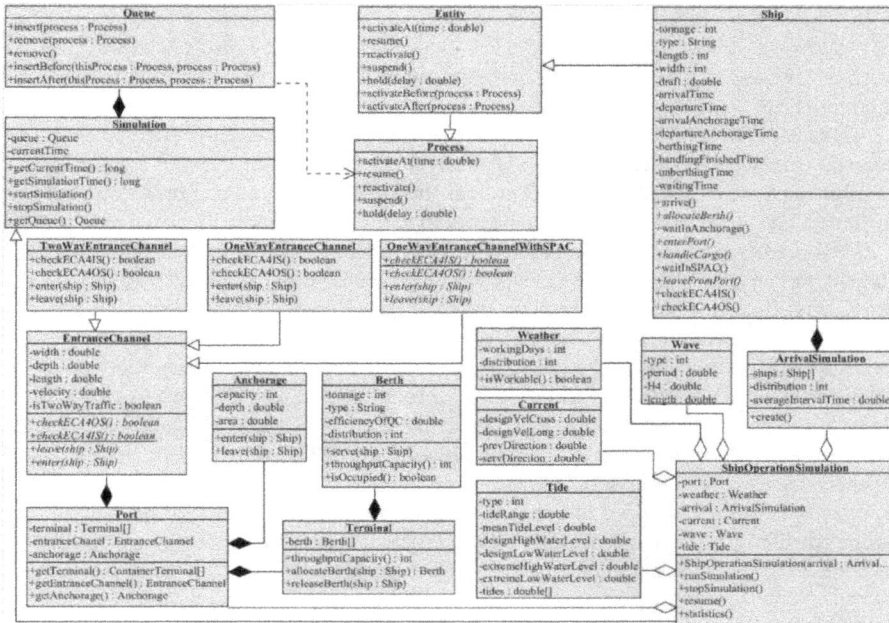

Figure 4.
Static structure diagram of classes implemented for ship traffic flow simulation.

other, such as activate, suspend, reactivate, and terminate a process. The *Entity* class represents the entities within a simulation which is derived from *Process* and has an independent thread of control associated with them at creation time, allowing them to convey the notion of activity necessary for participating in the simulation. The *Queue* class stores the inactive simulation processes within the simulation. The *Simulation* class derived from *Process*, which starts and stops a simulation, schedules the simulation processes: remove the process at the head of the queue and reactivate it. In simulation models, *Process*es are managed by a *Simulation* scheduler and are placed on a *Queue* (the event list).

SOS library is a collection of classes specialized for ship operation simulation, which are derived from the PIS library. Based on the components in a ship operation system, SOS library mainly consists of *Ship*, *Port*, *Terminal*, *Anchorage*, *EntranceChannel*, *ArrivalSimulation*, and *EntranceChannelSystem* classes as shown in **Figure 4**. The *Port*, *Terminal*, *Anchorage*, and *EntranceChannel* classes are permanent entity objects to provide services for *Ship* entities. The *ArrivalSimulation* class generates *Ship* entities randomly according to the ship arrival pattern. The *EntranceChannelSystem* class, a subclass of *Simulation*, schedules the processes of ship entities in and out of the port, makes a statistics analysis on simulation results, and outputs every ship's waiting time and berth's utilization ratio. The *Ship* class, a subclass of *Entity*, represents a ship entity, which is the core component of a process-interaction ship operation simulation model. The primary Java classes of PI-SMSO are illustrated in **Figure 4**, and it runs a simulation experiment as follows:

(1) Class *ShipOperationSimulation* is the control class of a simulation experiment. It initializes and activates the ship arrival process (Class *ArrivalSimulation*) and initializes port resources (e.g., Class *Port*, *Berth*, *Anchorage*, and *EntranceChannel*) and environmental conditions (e.g., Class *Current*, *Wave*, and *Tide*), then starts the simulation experiment.

(2) Class *ArrivalSimulation* generates a series of *Ship*s according to an inter-arrival time distribution [10, 14, 15]. For example, negative exponential distributions (NEDs) can be used to describe the arrival process [2], and its density function is $f(t) = \lambda e^{-\lambda t}$ (λ = arrival rate; t = inter-arrival time).

(3) Class *Ship* performs all activities of a ship as illustrated in **Figure 5** and records all necessary times related to performance measures.

Method *arrive* records the ship's arrival time and initializes its attributes (e.g., ship tonnage, dimensions, and cargo capacity).

Method *allocateBerth* requests for a berth according to berth allocation policy and queue priority [16], such as first-come-first-serve rule, longest/shortest processing time, and largest/smallest ship size. If a berth is assigned to this ship, the method records the time of berth availability and steps to Method *checkECA4IS*. Otherwise, this ship enters anchorage and waits (Method *waitInAnchorage*).

Method *checkECA4IS* checks weather, water depth, safety distance, and traffic situation for permission to enter channel as illustrated in **Figures 2** and **3**. In case a problem exists, the ship enters and waits in anchorage (Method *waitInAnchorage*). Otherwise, it steps to Method *enterPort*.

Method *waitInAnchorage* checks the availability of a free berth for no-berth-assigned ships (Method *allocateBerth*) and/or the availability of entrance channel

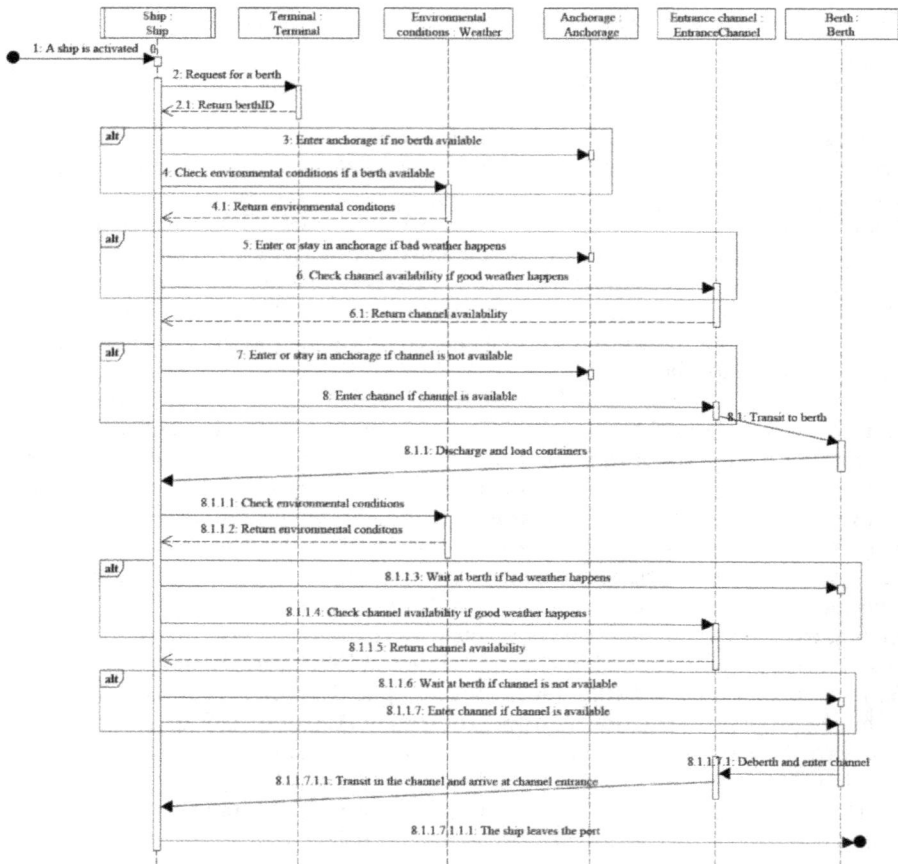

Figure 5.
UML sequence diagram for simulating ship operation in anchorage area, entrance channel, and berths.

for berth-assigned ships (Method *checkECA4IS*). Once all states meet safety requirements, the ship leaves anchorage, records the waiting time caused by berth occupation or channel unavailability, and enters Method *enterPort*.

Method *enterPort* transits this ship to the assigned berth via entrance channel and steps to Method *handleCargo*.

Method *handleCargo* discharges/loads cargoes from/onto the ship over a random berth service time and steps to Method *checkECA4OS*. For example, berth service time for each type of ship is fitted to an Erlang-k distribution [2, 17], and its probability density function is $f(t) = (k\mu)^k t^{k-1} e^{-k\mu t}/(k-1)!$ (μ = the number of ship services per day, and k = shape parameter).

Method *checkECA4OS* checks weather, water depth, safety distance, and traffic situation for permission to enter channel and leave the port. For one- and two-way channels without SPAC, if the *checkECA4OS* is "RURE," the outbound ship leaves the berth, travels through channel, and steps to Method *leaveFromPort*. For one-way channels with a SPAC, if the Channel *B* is available, the outbound ship leaves the berth, seizes an anchorage in SPAC, then travels through Channel *B*, and steps to Method *waitInSPAC*.

Method *waitInSPAC* records the time of arrival at SPAC, accommodates outbound ship mooring, and waits until Channel *A* is accessible. If Chanel *A* is accessible, the ship leaves the SPAC and enters Channel *A* and records the time of departure from SPAC, releases the occupied SPAC's anchorage, travels through Channel *A*, and steps to Method *leaveFromPort* finally.

Method *leaveFromPort* makes the ship entity exit the port system and records its departure time.

(4) Class *ShipOperationSimulation* finally stops the simulation experiment, updates the turnaround time and number of inbound and outbound ships, performs necessary statistical analysis, and outputs the values of port performance indicators.

3.3 Model verification and validation

This PI-SMSO model is verified and validated to confirm that it is correctly implemented with respect to the process of ship operation; we can use it to evaluate the port performance and then do more analysis. First, the model is developed through sub-models and individually examined by a subject-matter expert. Second, tracing approach comparing the simulation results with manual calculations is used to check the logic implemented in the model throughout the development of simulation model. Finally, we performed several simulation experiments based on real data on hand and compare the simulated values of key performance indicators with the real operational data, to check the accuracy of the model's representation of the real system [14, 18]. In this study, the key performance indicators we focus on are average turnaround time, average waiting time, average service time, waiting-time/service-time ratio, and berth utilization ratio; see Section 3.4.

3.4 Port performance indicators

Port performance measures the quality of service provided by ports, which are used to select an optimal design alternative [2, 19]. The most used indicators are (1) average turnaround time (ATAT) [20], (2) average waiting time (AWT) [4, 5, 21], (3) average service time (AST), (4) waiting-time/service-time ratio (AWT/AST) [21], and (5) berth utilization ratio (ρ) [21, 22].

The ATAT is the total time between ship arrival and departure, which portrays the port capability and the ability to provide services with high productivity and performance [5, 20]. The AST is the average value of the time between ship berthing and departure. The AWT is the average value of waiting time for the availability of a berth (AWTB) and the entrance channel (AWTC) [4, 5, 21]. AWT/AST is the ratio of the AWT to the AST, which is widely used as a measure of the service level of a terminal [21]. Berth utilization is the ratio of time the berth is occupied by vessels to the total time (1 year). High berth occupancy is a sign of congestion (>70%) and hence decline of services, while low berth occupancy signifies underutilization of resources (<50%) [22].

4. Case study

A specialized coal terminal in southern China serves local coal imports mainly from ports of Qingdao and Rizhao. Currently, this terminal has three berths and a one-way entrance channel, and its port throughputs is 16 million tons per year. According to its master planning, the throughputs of coal imports will be expected to increase to 20, 24.5, and 36 million tons per year in sequence as shown in **Table 1**, considering the rapid development of thermal power generation and steelmaking industries. Thus, as shown in **Tables 1** and **2**, more ships, even larger ships (e.g., 70,000- and 100,000-DWT bulk carriers), will call at this terminal, which leads to further pressures on the berths and entrance channel. Therefore, we initiate an evaluation of port system for Stages II, III, and IV, including entrance channel (see **Table 3**) and berths, to evaluate its performance (i.e., AWT/AST, AST, ATAT, AWTC, AWTB, and AWT, and the acceptable AWT/AST is 0.4) and identify the possible bottlenecks and then explore improvement strategies to improve its port performance based on a proactive long-term vision.

4.1 Simulation experiments

4.1.1 Stochastic characteristics

Table 4 lists the characteristics of environmental conditions including tides, waves, and current. We also collected historical data, such as the intervals between successive inbound ships, berth service times for each design ship, and port performance (ATAT, AWT, and AWT/AST). And we deduce that both intervals between ship arrivals and berth service time follow exponential distribution, and the parameters of each distribution (μ and λ) are listed in **Table 5**.

Item		Port scale				DWT of design ships calling at this berth (t)
		Stage I	Stage II	Stage III	Stage IV	
Number of berths	35,000-DWT	2	2	2	2	10,000, 20,000, 35,000
	50,000-DWT	1	1	1	1	20,000, 35,000, 50,000
	70,000-DWT			1	1	35,000, 50,000, 70,000
	100,000-DWT				1	50,000, 70,000, 100,000
Expected port throughput (10^4 t)		1600	2000	2450	3600	

Table 1.
The specifications of berths and their serving design ships and expected port throughputs.

Deadweight tonnage(t)	Overall length, Loa(m)	Molded breadth, B (m)	Static draft, T (m)	Actual load capacity, G (t)	Mean service time, t_s (h)
10,000	135	20.5	8.5	10,000	8.6
15,000	150	23.0	9.1	12,000	10.4
20,000	164	25.0	9.8	16,000	12.0
35,000	190	30.4	11.2	28,000	19.4
50,000	223	32.3	12.8	40,000	26.0
70,000	228	32.3	14.2	56,000	27.5
100,000	250	43.0	14.5	80,000	25.0

Table 2.
The specifications of the bulk ships calling at this coal terminal.

Channel type	Channel dimensions (m)				Port performance				
	Width	Depth	length	Navigable water level	AWT/AST	AWTC (h)	AWTB (h)	ATAT (h)
One-way traffic	178	15.6	8620	0.30	0.38	1.3	4.7	21.7

Table 3.
Existing entrance channel dimensions and its port performance.

4.1.2 Verification and validation

We run a series of simulation experiments based on **Tables 4** and **5** and compare the simulated results with real data from this coal terminal of Stage I to verify and validate the proposed simulation model. **Table 6** shows the simulation results for running the simulation model for 60 replications with each replication lasting for 1 year and gets the simulated average values of performance indicators. From the

Environmental condition	Item	Value
Tides	Tide type	Semidiurnal tide
	Average tidal range (m)	1.30
	Average level (m)	1.34
	Design high water level (m)	2.72
	Design low water level (m)	0.30
Waves	Height of $H_{4\%}$ (m)	2.0
	Period (s)	5.8
	Angle to channel (degree)	22.5
Current	Velocity (m/s)	0.66
	Angle to channel centerline (degree)	45
Adverse weather days (days/year)		20

Table 4.
Environmental conditions including tides, waves, and current.

Item	Unit	Value
1. *Port characteristics*		
-Berth specification		See **Table 1**
-Distribution of service time		Exponential distribution
-Mean service time per ship, μ	Hours	See **Table 2**
2. *Ship characteristics*		
-Distribution of inter-arrival times		Exponential distribution
-Mean inter-arrival time, $1/\lambda$		
• Stage I	Hours	8.3
• Stage II		7.1
• Stage III		9.2
• Stage IV		8.3
-Ship specifications		See Table 3
3. *Simulation parameters*		
-Simulation time, T_{sim}	Hours	365 × 24
-Simulation repetitions		
• One-way channel		20
• Two-way channel		40
• One-way channel with a SPAC		40

Table 5.
Simulation parameters of simulation model for this coal terminal.

Performance indicator	Actual data	Simulation results	Difference percentage (%)
AWT/AST	0.38	0.36	−5.4
AWTC (h)	1.3	1.21	−6.9
AWTB (h)	4.7	4.43	−5.7
AST (h)	15.79	14.77	−6.5
ATAT (h)	23.6	23.21	−1.6
ρ	0.52	0.50	−4.2

Table 6.
Comparison of simulation results and actual data.

results from **Table 6**, we find that all average values of simulation results lie within 7% difference from the actual values, which means the established simulation model built for this terminal is considered to be close to the actual system.

4.2 Results and discussions

4.2.1 Evaluation of current berths and channel system

We evaluate the performances of the berths and entrance channel system for Stages II, III, and IV using the proposed simulation model, provided that the dimensions of entrance channel remain unchanged. **Table 7** shows the channel dimensions, the values of port performance indicators for Stages II, III, and IV.

Item		Stage I	Stage II	Stage III	Stage IV
Entrance channel	Channel type	One-way channel			
	Width (m)	178	178	180	224
	Depth (m)	15.6	15.6	17.1	17.6
	Length (m)	8620	8620	9810	10,200
Port performance	AWT/AST	0.38	1.15	0.41	0.63
	ρ	0.52	0.62	0.55	0.58
	ATAT	23.6	35.4	28.9	39.4
	AST	15.7	15.6	18.6	22.2
	AWT	6.0	17.9	7.6	14.0
	AWTC	1.3	1.8	1.5	1.9
	AWTB	4.7	16.1	6.0	12.1

Table 7.
The channel dimensions and measures of port performance for Stages I, II, III, and IV.

(1) In Stage II, the annual port throughput is expected to hit 20 million tons of coal. If the berths and channel dimensions remain unchanged, the AWT/AST is as high as 1.15 beyond the accepted AWT/AST of 0.4 as shown in **Table 7**. So the terminal will be running with an extremely low efficiency, which leads to higher vessel wait. Note that 90% of the AWT (17.9 h) is spent waiting for the availability of a berth (AWTB = 16.1 h). Therefore, it seems that more berths should be provided in order to improve port performance.

(2) In Stage III, the expected port throughput is 24.5 million tons of coal; the channel is still a one-way channel, but a new 70,000-DWT berth is built to accommodate deeper-draft bulk carriers. Thus, for serving larger ships, the entrance channel has to be expanded as shown in **Table 7**: the channel depth being expanded to 17.1 m, channel width being expanded to 180 m, and channel length being expanded to 9810 m. Meanwhile, by building a new berth, the AWT/AST falls to 0.41 from 1.15, the ATAT falls to 28.9 h from 35.4 h, and the AWTB is only 6.0 h with a decrease of 10 h from 16.1 h. Therefore, in Stage III, the terminal with a one-way channel will be operated with an acceptable service level without expanding one-way to two-way channel.

(3) In Stage IV, the expected port throughput is 37 million tons of coal; the channel is still a one-way channel, but a new berth is built to serve the 100,000-DWT bulk carriers. So to serve 100,000-DWT ships, the dimensions of one-way channels are expanded to 17.55 m depth, 224 m width, and 10,200 m length. Meanwhile, the AWT/AST is 0.63, higher than the accepted service level of 0.4. And the ships take 86% of the AWT to wait for the availability of a berth. Therefore, expansion strategies are needed to improve port performance in Stage IV.

4.2.2 Improvement strategies and their performance

According to simulation results and analysis, we propose three types of improvement strategies for Stages II and IV, including setting a ship-passing anchorage (SPAC), expanding into a two-way traffic channel (E2TWC), and building new berths (BNB), and the detailed parameters are given in **Table 8**.

We run the simulation models to get simulation results for all proposed alternatives and to explore the performance improvements as follows.

Stage	Strategy	Entrance channel type	Berths (DWT, t)
II	SPAC	One-way with SPAC	35,000, 35,000, 50,000
	E2TWC	Two-way	
	BNB	One-way	35,000, 35,000, 50,000, 70,000
IV	SPAC	One-way with SPAC	35,000, 35,000, 50,000, 70,000, 100,000
	E2TWC	Two-way	

Table 8.
The details of the proposed improvement strategies.

Strategy	Entrance channel type	AWT/AST	
		AWT/AST	Percentage decrease (%)
Current	One-way	1.15	/
SPAC	One-way with SPAC	0.77	33
E2TWC	Two-way	0.56	51
BNB	One-way	0.25	79

Table 9.
The AWT/AST between current and proposed alternatives for Stage II.

Strategy	Entrance channel type	AWT/AST		Construction cost of channel (10⁴ CNY)
		AWT/AST	Percentage decrease (%)	
Current	One-way	0.63	/	0
SPAC	One-way with SPAC	0.37	40.8	0
E2TWC	Two-way	0.35	44.2	2200

Table 10.
The AWT/AST and channel construction costs between current and proposed alternatives for Stage IV.

As shown in **Table 9**, for Stage II, when comparing the current AWT/AST of 1.15, the AWT/ASTs for SPAC, E2TWC, and BNB strategies are 0.77, 0.56, and 0.25. Therefore, strategies SPAC, E2TWC, and BNB all improve the service level, and the BNB strategy is the best way. However, according to the required AWT/AST of 0.4, only the BNB strategy by building a new 70,000-DWT berth is practicable in Stage II.

Similarly, we also collect the AWT/ASTs for both SPAC and E2TWC strategies in Stage IV and list them in **Table 10**. As shown in **Table 10**, the AWT/ASTs for SPAC and E2TWC strategies are 0.37 and 0.35, so that both SPAC and E2TWC strategies are most effective alternatives in Stage IV from point view of AWT/AST. However, considering the costs of these two strategies, we suggest the strategy SPAC as a practical alternative for Stage IV.

Finally, we list the proposed entrance channel and berths for Stages II, III, and IV in **Table 11**. Therefore, this application shows that the implemented simulation model is helpful for evaluating the capacity of entrance channel, identifying the bottlenecks in port system, and determining an optimal improvement strategy effectively for improving port performance.

Stage	Entrance channel type	Berths (DWT, t)	
		Master plan	Proposed
I	One-way	35,000, 35,000, 50,000	35,000, 35,000, 50,000
II			35,000, 35,000, 50,000, 70,000
III		35,000, 35,000, 50,000, 70,000	
IV	One-way with a SPAC	35,000, 35,000, 50,000, 70,000, 100,000	

Table 11.
The proposed entrance channel and berths for Stages II, III, and IV.

5. Conclusions

Increases in ship size and number lead to further pressures on the entrance channel to minimize time in port. Moreover, the design of an entrance channel system is a complex challenge, considering the stochastic environment and time-consuming calculations. Therefore, we develop a process-interaction-based simulation model for ship operation (PI-SMSO) using Java programming language, to help the designers to evaluate the capacity of entrance channel and then to determine when to expand the channel and to select the dimensions of the expanded channel. The PI-SMSO simulates ship operation in the entrance channel including one- or two-way traffic channel, or a one-way channel with a ship-passing anchorage, and outputs the values of the selected port performance indicators. Finally, we apply the PI-SMSO to a Chinese coal terminal to explore its bottlenecks and to evaluate available improvement strategies for further development of this coal terminal. And the results prove that the implemented PI-SMSO performs well in evaluating the capacity of entrance channels and identifying the possible bottlenecks of a port system. Therefore, the proposed PI-SMSO provides a reference for government agencies involved with the design of port systems.

Moreover, the architecture PI-SMSO includes other water areas, such as outside anchorage area, maneuvering basin, and mooring basin; we can apply PI-SMSO to evaluate the capacity of water areas of a port. Besides, further researches will focus on optimizing the general layout of a port as a whole by integrating ship operation simulation in water area with port operation simulation in land area, considering the water areas and land areas are interlinked.

Acknowledgements

This research is supported by the National Natural Science Foundation of China (Grant No. 51579035), Science and Technology Foundation of Liaoning Province, China (Grant No. 20170540150), and Support High-Level Talents Innovation and Entrepreneurship Projects, Dalian, China (Grant No. 2016RQ024).

Author details

Tang Guolei[1*] and Qi Yue[2]

1 Dalian University of Technology, Dalian, China

2 Transport Planning and Research Institute, Ministry of Transport, Beijing, China

*Address all correspondence to: tangguolei@outlook.com

IntechOpen

References

[1] Design Code of General Layout of Seaport, JTS 165-2013. China: Ministry of Transport of the People's Republic of China. Beijing; 2014

[2] PIANC MarCom Working Group 121. Harbour approach channels—Design Guidelines. MarCom Report 121; 2014

[3] Lardas M. The Port of Houston. United States: Arcadia Publishing; 2013

[4] Tang G, Wang W, Guo Z, Yu X, Wang B. Simulation-based optimization for generating the dimensions of a dredged coastal entrance channel. Simulation: Transactions of the Society for Modeling and Simulation International. 2014;**90**(9):1059-1070. DOI: 10.1177/0037549714540954

[5] Tang GL, Guo ZJ, Yu XH, Song XQ, Du PC. SPAC to improve port performance for seaports with very long one-way entrance channels. Journal of Waterway, Port, Coastal, and Ocean Engineering. 2014;**140**:04014011:1-13. DOI: 10.1061/(ASCE) WW.1943-5460.0000248

[6] Angela Y. Two-Way Channel Investment at Guangzhou port. 2015. http://www.joc.com/port-news/two-way-channel-investment-guangzhou-port_20150527.html. [Accessed: October 1, 2015]

[7] Tang G, Wang W, Song X, Guo Z, Yu X, Qiao F. Effect of entrance channel dimensions on berth occupancy of container terminals. Ocean Engineering. 2016;**117**(1):174-187. DOI: 10.1016/j.oceaneng.2016.03.047

[8] Groenveld R. Ship Traffic Simulation Study Port Extension Maasvlakte 2 of the Port of Rotterdam. Portugal: Estoril; 2006

[9] Song XQ, Zhang YC, Tang GL, Wang WY. Affection of turnout anchorage on throughput capacity of fairway in coastal bulk port. Journal of Waterway, Port, Coastal, and Ocean Engineering. 2012;**11**:124-127

[10] Quy NM, Vrijling JK, van Gelder PHAJM. Risk- and simulation-based optimization of channel depths: Entrance channel of Cam Pha Coal Port. Simulation. 2008;**84**:41-55. DOI: 10.1177/0037549708088958

[11] Bruce E. Thinking in Java. 4th ed. New York: Prentice Hall PTR; 2006

[12] Liu BH. Object-Oriented Modeling and Simulation. Beijing: Tsinghua University Press; 2011

[13] Holmevik JR. Compiling Simula: A historical study of technological genesis. IEEE Annals of the History of Computing. 1994;**16**(4):25-37. DOI: 10.1109/85.329756

[14] Banks J, Carson JS, Nelson BL, Nicol DM. Discrete event system simulation. 3rd ed. Upper Saddle River, NJ: Prentice Hall; 2001

[15] Shabayek AA, Yeung WW. A simulation model for the Kwai Chung container terminals in Hong Kong. European Journal of Operational Research. 2002;**140**(1):1-11. DOI: 10.1016/S0377-2217(01)00216-8

[16] Wanke P. Ship-berth link and demurrage costs. evaluating different allocation policies and queue priorities via simulation. Pesquisa Operacional. 2011;**31**(1):113-134. DOI: 10.1590/S0101-74382011000100008

[17] Guo Z, Wang W, Song X, Tang G. A new method to measure the passing capacity of coastal waterway considering service level by simulation computation. Journal of the Eastern Asia Society for Transportation Studies.

2010;**8**:2272-2282. DOI: 10.11175/
eastpro.2009.0.422.0

[18] Kotachi M, Rabadi G, Obeid
MF. Simulation modeling and analysis
of complex port operations with
multimodal transportation. Procedia
Computer Science. 2013;**20**:229-
234. DOI: https://doi.org/10.1016/j.
procs.2013.09.266

[19] Yu X, Tang G, Guo Z, Song X, Yu J.
Performance comparison of real-time
yard crane dispatching strategies at
nontransshipment container terminals.
Mathematical Problems in Engineering.
2018:1-15. DOI: 10.1155/2018/5401710

[20] Rabadi G, Pinto CA, Talley W,
Arnaout JP. Port recovery from security
incidents: A simulation approach. In:
Risk Management in Port Operations,
Logistics and Supply-Chain Security.
London: Informa Law from Routledge;
2007;**5**:83-94

[21] Said GA, El-Horbaty EM. A
Simulation Modeling Approach
for Optimization of Storage Space
Allocation in Container Terminal. 2015.
CoRR, abs/1501.06802

[22] Mwasenga H. Port performance
indicators: A case of Dar es Salaam
port. In: Proceedings of UNCTAD, Ad
Hoc Expert Meeting on Assessing Port
Performance. Geneva, Switzerland;
2012

The Proposal for Modeling Methodology for Enterprise Content Management (ECM) Systems: Modeling Tools Selection

Jan Trąbka

Abstract

Content management is one of the strategic directions of the ICT development in modern enterprises. This trend is spurred by the increasing amount of data, information, and explicit knowledge (that is content) whose characteristic features are lack of structure and multimediality. A dynamically growing market of ECM platforms, defined as the set of components and technologies used for managing content in any given area of the company, has emerged. Researchers focusing on ECM agree that the current aspect of content management is much more recognizable in the business practice rather than the theoretical and methodological ECM toolkit as a separate discipline of IS. This chapter presents the main elements of the author's methodology of modeling the enterprise that is preparing for the ECM platform implementation. The working name of this methodology is enterprise content management modeling method (ECM3). The modeling methodology is understood as a set of assumptions and perspectives of building the enterprise model, analytical tools to create it, and stages of the completion of the analytical process. The chapter presents the assumptions of methodology, selected analytical tools as well as practical examples from the actual ECM implementation.

Keywords: enterprise content management (ECM), enterprise content management modeling method, content workflow, organizational structure, locational structure, BPMN, UML

1. Introduction

Undoubtedly, the biggest challenge over the next few years that IT community will have to face is the exponential increase in the amount of data processed [1]. The IDC analysts quoted above estimate that 80% of data is produced by enterprises. The form of the data is significantly changing too with the domination of unstructured data, i.e., documents of various types and formats, e.g., announcements, e-mails, messages, sound and image recordings. Approximately, 90% of the data processed is unstructured [2]. This unstructured character of data has been encapsulated in the notion of content managed by processes and technologies which at the beginning of the century were collectively called enterprise content management (ECM). Current ECM definition, created and updated by Association for

Information and Image Management (AIIM), reads: "it is a dynamic combination of strategies, methods, and tools used to capture, manage, store, preserve, and deliver information supporting key organizational processes through its entire lifecycle" [3]. Today, ECM is one of the strategic directions of the ICT development in modern enterprises. A market comparison of ECM tools and ERP systems is a good indicator of ECM's popularity and dynamic growth. For the last couple of years, ERP systems have been the most important component of enterprise infrastructure. "Research and Markets" agency reports show that the estimated compound annual growth rate (CAGR) for global ECM market revenue for 2018–2022 is going to be 15.51% [4]. According to the same source, CAGR for the global ERP market for 2017–2025 is going to be 7.4% [5].

ECM is also a growing research area. Simons and Van Brocke in their study on the current position of ECM in the IS discipline stress its strategic and integrative character. The authors compared ECM development dynamics in technology and implementation practice to its theoretical and methodological aspects and pointed to evident deficiencies in the latter ones [6].

The author of this chapter has also encountered the problem in his research. Being a scientist and academic teacher engaged in IS analyses and design (mainly ERP, workflow, and BI), he participated in a project of ECM system implementation in a large Polish enterprise operating in the medical field. As a member of the analytical team, he was responsible for the preimplementation analysis and supervised the stage of the final solution's design once a supplier had been selected. From the project's beginning, one could see a blank area in the sector of methodologies and analytical tools dedicated to ECM systems. General methodologies, known from theory and practice, met the ECM requirements only to some extent. For the author, a business project transformed into research whose aim was to create an integrated modeling methodology for ECM systems implementation in an organization. The methodology was given a working name of enterprise content management modeling methodology (ECM3). The research adopted the design science research methodology approach. The methodology and research process used as well as the project's details will be presented in Section 3. ECM3 methodology development was initiated with the recognition of current ECM strategies and technologies state of the art, and indication of a set of tactical perspectives on an enterprise (based on the project experience). This initial stage was realized and described in the author's article [7]. The perspectives and ECM3 methodology's characteristics have been briefly characterized in Section 4. The core subject of the chapter is to present the second stage of the project, namely the process of modeling tool selection regarding individual perspectives. Its main part (Section 5) is devoted to analytical tool selection for each of the four key perspectives: content, processes, and organizational and locational structures. Conclusion contains a summary of the selection process' results and presents next steps of ECM3 methodology design.

2. ECM strategies and technologies: short overview

ECM platform technological characteristics and evolution were extensively described in the author's articles [7, 8]. In this section, we will focus on the technological aspect driving the whole ECM area, which proved to be a great challenge when creating an analysis methodology and modeling an organization implementing an ECM system.

ECM systems are not monoliths but sets of components and technologies building the foundation for creation of functional modules supporting any processes and content collections in an enterprise. These characteristics are reflected in the literary and practical name of the platform—ECM [8]. The set of technologies which the platform embraces is huge and dynamically growing. This dynamics is reflected in a comparison of main ECM components performed by Gartner's analysts and published in the yearly "Quadrant for Enterprise Content Management" reports. In 2015, the components list included: document management, web content management, records management, image-processing applications, social content, content workflow, and extended components [9]. A year later, the set was extended with analytics/BI and packaged apps and integration [10]. In the same report, Gartner's analysts put forward their own integrative and elastic definition of ECM—"[it] is a set of services and micro-services, embodied either as an integrated product suite or as separate applications that share common APIs and repositories, to exploit diverse content types, and serve multiple constituencies and numerous use cases across an organization." This points to the persisting tendency to adapt other technologies to ECM services. For the methodology created, ECM3 is an indicator of a large and constantly widening range of objects and processes modeled, a range not required for other class systems.

As far as strategies are concerned, there are a few approaches to the ECM domain which have been used for the ECM3 development. The first is "a framework for ECM research" proposed by Tyrväinen and others [11]. The framework consists of four strategic and integrated perspectives: content, technology, processes, and enterprise. The perspectives became a starting point for searching for tactical sections of ECM3 enterprise modeling. "A Unified Content Strategy" (UCS) is the second approach, which changed the outlook on unstructured content as an element extremely difficult to manage [12]. Its assumptions are very much used in content perspective modeling (see Section 5.1). More detailed characteristics and other strategies used in ECM3 methodology building can be found in [7].

3. Research methodology

ECM3 methodology is created in accordance with a research rigor consisting in solving problems observed in a real-life project of ECM platform implementation in a large organization. The case study has become a place of problem identification where the solution is developed on the basis of the discipline's theoretical knowledge and the author's experience. Close cooperation between the researchers and the business people at most of the research stages will prove to be of key importance. The following sections thoroughly discuss the assumptions and research process of the design science research approach and provide a brief characteristic of the organization researched as well as the assumptions of the ECM platform implementation project.

3.1 Research process

The ECM3 methodology components' (perspectives, tools, procedures) building process has been conducted on the basis of design science research methodology (DSRM) for information systems research [13]. DSRM consists in solving problems (often real business world ones) on the basis of an existing theory which is implemented, tested, and then modified according to researchers' experience and intuition [14]. Implementation and testing occur within organizations interested in utilization of the solution created. The method is characterized by close cooperation between the business world and researchers [15] as well as the problem-solving process' iteration and agility [16]. DSRM approach adopted in the article was supported by an analysis of an organization facing the challenges of ECM platform implementation (the organization and project have been described in the following section). The use case analysis contained not only the place of implementation, testing, and verification processes but also the source of the research problem definition and aim. The DSRM process proposed by Havner et al. [17] consists of six steps: problem identification, definition of solution's objectives, design and development, demonstration, evaluation, and communication. The process used to create ECM3 is presented in **Figure 1**.

3.2 The organization and project's characteristics

To discuss the research problem and its solution developed correspondingly to the process shown in **Figure 1**, the organization and project's assumptions have been presented below. The enterprise subject to this research is one of the biggest medical diagnostics laboratories network in Poland (the company's board agreed to publish information without disclosing the company's name). Its organizational structure consists of 140 laboratories and over 600 collection stations which sum together to over 1000 organizational units. The laboratories perform 28 million tests a year and the enterprise employs about 4000 people. As the network covers the whole country, its organizational structure has been divided into eight regions which are evenly spread across the territory of Poland. Each of the regions is divided into branches operating in one or two voivodeships (Polish administrative areas). A branch is made

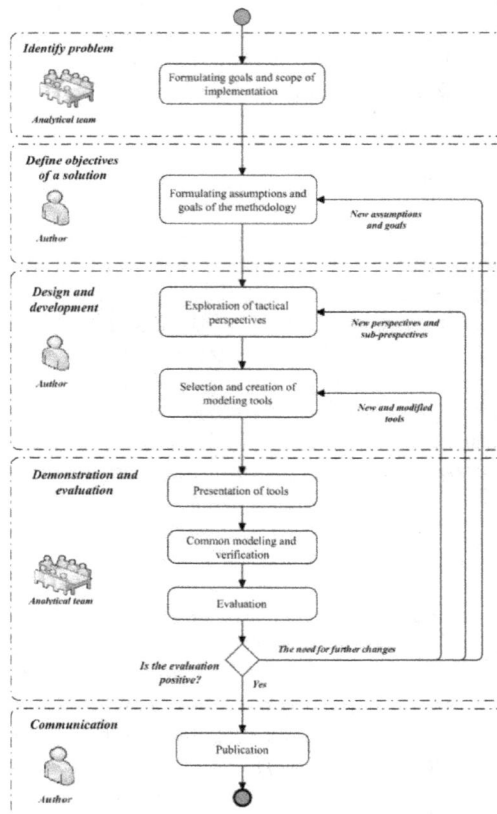

Figure 1.
The research process used in ECM3 methodology creation (based on DSRM).

up of a couple of laboratories located in bigger cities. Each laboratory is divided into laboratory units providing services for tens of sample collection stations. The company has a certified quality management system ISO 9001 as well as branch certificates PN-EN ISO 15189:2008 and PN-EN ISO/IEC 17025:2005. The territorial scope of the enterprise and the number of documents (200,000 documents a year in office circulation and 150,000 in quality management system) flowing between the organization's units gave rise to the board's decision to start a project aimed at selection and implementation of an ECM platform as a central electronic system for document and case circulation. The project was divided into three main areas: the incoming and outgoing correspondence called office document circulation, financial document circulation and approval (purchase and business trip invoices, etc.), and quality management documentation (with the required creation, acceptance, and distribution processes). The project started with a preimplementation analysis performed to build the organization's model and define its functional and nonfunctional requirements. The analysis outcome was a key to carry out the procedure of ECM platform supplier selection. Next stage consisted in developing a solution project, which was a task assigned to the researched company's analytical team and the contractor's analysts. The two abovementioned stages took 1 year. Currently, the project is in the end phase of implementation.

As has been mentioned in the introduction, the chapter's author was engaged in the project as an external expert for the analysis and design stages. In the course of these, a research gap was diagnosed—lack of ECM-platform-dedicated methodological and tool support. In the iterative research process (**Figure 1**), the author identified other significant analytical perspectives and selected tools for their modeling. The results were periodically demonstrated, tested, and corrected. The final results have been described further in the chapter.

4. ECM3 methodology: assumptions and tactical perspectives

Naming the operational analytical tools (that is, modeling languages or independent notations) is the second stage of the methodology's building. The first one is discovering the perspectives we are going to use to present a real object in order to make the model created complete and comprehensible so it can become the basis for designing new or improved objects (in our case, ECM systems). The author making use of the research process described in Section 3.1 finalized this stage and published its results in "A proposal for an ECM systems modeling method – defining tactical perspectives — lesson learnt from a case study" [7]. In the article, he identified the ECM3 methodology for the first time and pointed to its strategic attributes: integration and accessibility. In the course of the research process, there were presented six main perspectives on an organization preparing for ECM platform implementation, namely: content, process, organizational structure, locational structure, business rules, and IT environment. The perspectives are integrated, which means each of them directly or indirectly corresponds to the rest. The connections are so strong that it is practically impossible to model a perspective without considering at least one of the others. The processes perspective may serve here as a good example as it can hardly be modeled without roles, i.e., employees or groups of employees performing particular tasks. Information on roles and individual employees comes from organizational structure. When modeling a process whose core element is the question where the role is physically, we need to take into consideration the locational perspective. A typical process of financial document workflow is yet another example—without being familiar with the data structure the document contains, it is difficult to plan

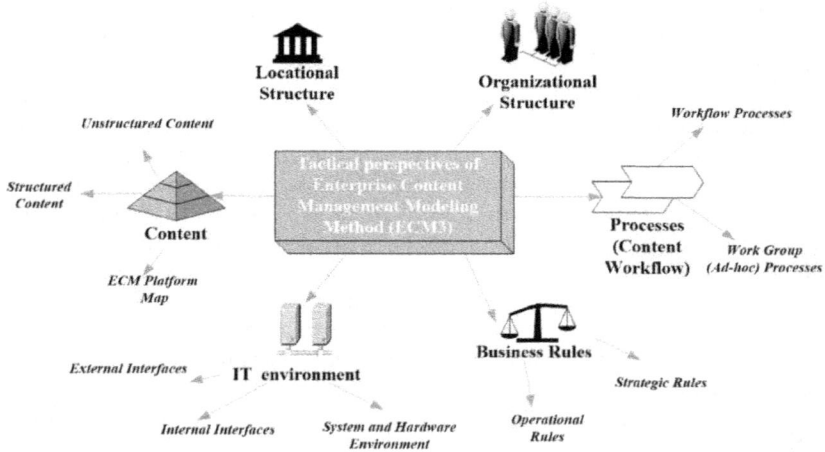

Figure 2.
ECM3 methodology's perspectives and subperspectives.

next steps of its circulation. In this case, we need to use the content perspective, which is the document's internal structure. When describing the mechanism of the presented ECM3 tactical perspectives integration, one should emphasize that it is also used to examine the completeness and conciseness of the whole organization model. The mechanism is used in many methodologies, just to mention the structured ones [18].

The ECM3 perspectives are frequently so complex that they have been divided into subperspectives. The most compound content perspective has been split into three subperspectives: unstructured content, structured content, and ECM platforms map. Each of these represents content in different forms, which is the reason why tool selection will be determined on the subperspective level. More detailed characteristics of the perspectives, their subperspectives, and the process of analytical tool selection have been presented in the next section.

A set of ECM3 methodology perspectives and subperspectives has been depicted in **Figure 2**.

The ECM3 methodology's accessibility is vital when it comes to modeling tool selection. The accessibility consists in the fact that it uses standard, generally available, and open languages or modeling notations like Business Process Model and Notation (BPMN) [19] or the Unified Modeling Language (UML) [20], both of which are completely free. It also allows us to access multiple IT tools, commercial and free ones, in which we can model in compliance with the indicated standards. The author considered using commercial methodologies like ARIS or BPMS in case of the organizational and locational perspectives. The results were discussed in [16].

5. Key ECM3 perspectives modeling tool selection

Modeling tool selection was the next step taken after identifying tactical perspectives of the organization modeled. The project subject to this research contains descriptions of perspectives recognized in to date IS theory and practice, such as data and processes, and ECM-dedicated perspectives discovered in the course of project, namely content and the organizational and locational structures. The process of perspective identification and tool selection was asynchronous (for the perspectives) and iterative. The asynchrony was largely caused by the project's scope covering the three areas to be supported by the ECM platform: office and financial documents flow as well as quality management. The research started with an analysis of the document types, tracking their source, authors, and flow in the organization. One may say it began with the classical structural approach focusing on data (currently on content) and their processing. The works started simultaneously in all areas. The stage exposed significant differences in the importance and time devoted to modeling individual perspectives. The office and financial areas were dominated by the process perspective (documents are structurally simpler, e.g., an invoice) where processes comprise of more steps and alternative courses. The quality management area was dominated by the content perspective as the documents processed there were more structurally and semantically varied. The other ECM3 perspectives were identified later in the project. The order in which the perspectives appeared does not denote their final chronology or significance in ECM3 methodology.

The modeling tool selection was based on the criteria of their simplicity and comprehensibility for business people. Modeling is part of the business analysis stage supposed to give a clear view of the organization to be used later in IT tool design and implementation processes. Business users are data carriers; analysts provide tools and translate business knowledge to the model's formal language. One should remember that the model created needs to be verified and accepted by business people, which can only be done when it is intelligible and clearly expressed.

The sections present tool selection for four ECM3 perspectives: content, processes, and the organizational and locational structures. The other perspectives will be described with the progress of ECM3 methodology research.

5.1 Content perspective

Content is collection of structured and unstructured data, information, and explicit knowledge available in the electronic format (e.g., database records, digitalized documents, electronic documents, e-mails, messages sent through social media, or sound and image recordings) as well as the traditional format (i.e., paper or microfilm) [8]. Metadata used to describe content so that it can be later identified and categorized are the core of content management. In the DMS systems era, metadata were used to give document identification and library attributes to make it more easily searched for in electronic repositories. The original document in electronic form (scan, sound recording, or image) was attached to the set of metadata it was described by. We were able to manage the document as a whole but had no access to its actual contents. Today, when metadata can also carry document's semantic content, content management goes further—guided by the unified content strategy [12], we try to divide the document into semantic fragments and thus choose "information products" over uniform document. Information product can be further split into components consisting of elements. Such division allows us to provide access to semantic contents of a document and consequently make it reusable and adaptable. Information product (initial document) can be completely described (including its content) with metadata and stored directly in a database (not as an attachment in file system). One may conclude that currently content management is a process of converting unstructured content to semi- and fully structured one.

The ECM3 methodology content perspective has been divided into the following subperspectives: structured content, unstructured content, and ECM platform map. The first two require very similar tools, while the third one includes synthetic (bird's eye) view on all content resources available on an ECM platform. Modeling this aspect allows us to organize an organization's content resources (create its repository) and plan which content areas and other ECM system's functionalities will be available to individual groups of employees.

5.1.1 Structured and unstructured content subperspectives

XML is the basic tool used to convert a document into information products. At the stage of design and implementation, all types of content are stored and processed as XML documents and schemas. The question arises whether XML could also be used at the analytical stage to model the shape of final documents meeting ECM system's needs. The author's project experience demonstrates it is possible and effective and can be applied, especially to documents of simple (one- or two-level) semantic structure, e.g., research procedures, instructions, quality manuals, which were all present in the quality management area of the project subject to this chapter. XML's definite advantage is the fact it has clear rules for tag interpretation and use in document's structure projection. The rules can be easily understood and learned by every business participant. Additionally, one can create tag names in the organization's business language. Creating an XML content model for a given type of quality document consists in indicating text fragments constituting the model's components and elements (in accordance with UCS) and equipping these with structural and semantical tags. The task can be performed directly in a text editor, e.g., MS Word, when analyzing examples of documents in their original form. The abovementioned MS Word is provided with special XML schema (.xsd) interpretation options and facilitates placing XML tags in the document's text. A document's analysis starts with selecting fragments of text and giving them tag names. On this basis, an analyst creates a draft of XML schema which is next attached to the document and the tagging process is repeated. XML schema is completed after a few iterations and builds foundations for respective structures in the ECM repository. These XML functionalities can be found in standard Word application since the 2007 release. **Figure 3** presents a research procedure document filled with XML schema tags.

When the documents modeled are relationally much more complex and their attributes are to be used in computational processes, we need to use other modeling techniques. In case of the project, the documents were contractor agreements, e.g., premises lease contracts. The main purpose here was to extract from the text any measurable, quantitative, or valuable attributes to build automatic mechanisms for controlling cost settlements ensuing from the agreements and, further, for their booking. Documents of this type were modeled in the entity-relationship (ER) notation and mirrored as relational data models. Less important descriptive parameters, such as rights and responsibilities of the parties, could be stored in separate metadata sets or left in the document original's scan saved as the agreements attribute. The modeling was performed following the entity relationship diagram (ERD) [18, 21], whose construction principles are extremely easy to convey to the analytical team members not acquainted with IT environment. In an exemplary document of premises lease contract, the objects specified were contract, contract subject, and premises. Next step consisted in determining the relations and attributes of individual objects. Project experience shows that employees of financial, audit, or administrative departments are well acquainted with the data relations concept as it is present in everyday use systems like ERP, CRM, or BI. Consequently, they are familiar with notions of foreign key or 1:N relations, and similar. **Figure 4** depicts a relational model of a car lease contract.

Alternatively, one can build conceptual models of documents such as contracts, using the class diagram belonging to UML [22]. Comparison of the two techniques was presented in [21]. An interesting approach to modeling advanced XML

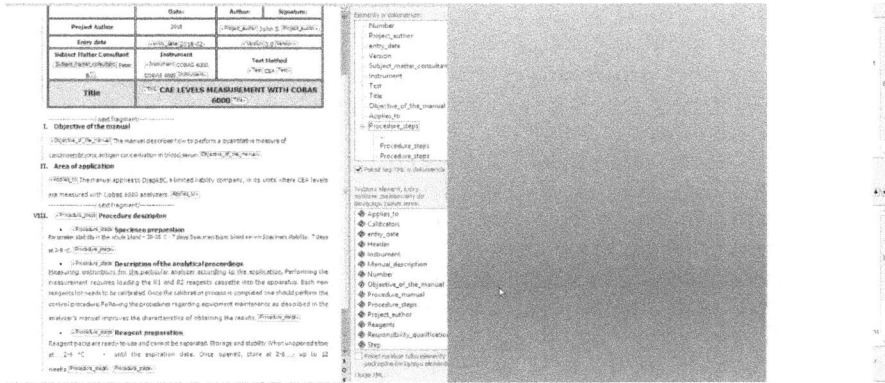

Figure 3.
Content modeling using XML and MS Word 2007.

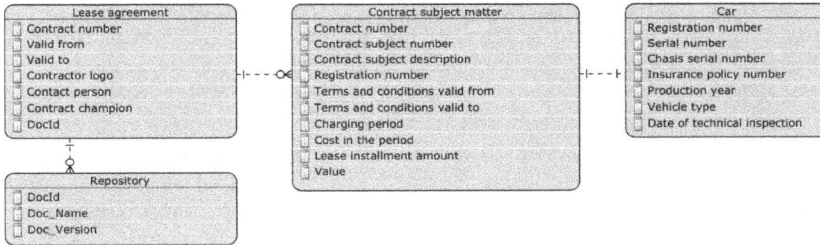

Figure 4.
Relational model of a car lease contract (ERD notation).

documents was described in [23] where UML, and in particular, class diagram were used. However, the author's project experience shows that when modeling content perspective ERD notation is more intuitive and easier to use.

ECM3 methodology also recognizes the perspective of structured content used in ECM platforms in the form of lists (or dictionaries) gathering contractors, employees, organizational units, etc. These are ordered, most often relational data which can be best organized with ERD or class diagram notations.

5.1.2 ECM platform map subperspective

ECM platform is a place where each of the organization's employees gets access to important content (stored in the ECM system's repository). They can initiate or realize tasks in the processes of document creation and circulation—like correspondence, invoices, settlements of delegations, or quality procedures, and at the same time have access to social functionalities—notice boards, newsletters, forums, blogs, wikibases (collectively called social content components).

ECM platforms are equipped with web content management (WCM) component (inherited from CMS systems). It allows us to create on an ECM platform a structure of internal sites and, in this way, give individual employees the access to various areas and functionalities of the platform. Sites can have different access configurations to the repository, processes, or social content. The ECM repository should be divided into subject areas (referred to as subjects further in the chapter) which facilitate giving the right to create, modify, or view content. In the project, the repository was divided into the following subjects: Board, HR, Quality, IT, Technology, Microbiology, etc. Each of the subjects was assigned an editor in the form of the company's department overlooking the particular area of the enterprise. The stage of ECM platform design proliferates in site models for individual departments/subjects or groups of employees. The sites share the repository's subject areas. Each of the single site's models states who it is designed for, which subjects it will use, and what social functionalities it will have. It is a multifocused task whose components are nonhomogeneous, abstract, and informal. In the project, the technique used for site modeling was mind mapping. Mind mapping diagrams are very little formalized (they are based on just a few simple rules)—when used as tools for creative or project work, one should use their own symbols and colors [24]. Business users know mind mapping from trainings on creative thinking or project management and the technique is used by many in their day-to-day work [25]. Mind mapping as a tool for website content design was described by Deer [26]. According to him, content mapping is a "visual technique that will help you organize and understand the content of a website" and is "similar to mind maps, but it's focused on a site's content" [26].

In the project, mind maps were used to design sites for individual groups of employees or the entire organization. Single groups formed the roots of the mind mapping diagram (consequently, the site's physical name on the ECM platform was the same as the group's). **Figure 5** presents an example of a site dedicated to Laboratory Managers. The site had a few groups of employees and access to various content areas in the repository and social functions the group needed. Mind mapping notation is so simple and intuitive that ECM platform site modeling can be passed directly to target employees just providing them with the pattern. IT tools include many programs, both free and commercial, that support mind mapping. CASE-type packages also offer mind mapping diagrams as a complete analytical tool, as does the Visual Paradigm package used by the author [27].

5.2 Content processes perspective

The processes responsible for creation, modification, distribution (as well as other stages of content lifecycle) of content processed in ECM systems have been named "Content Processes" or "Content Workflow" [28]. Literature research

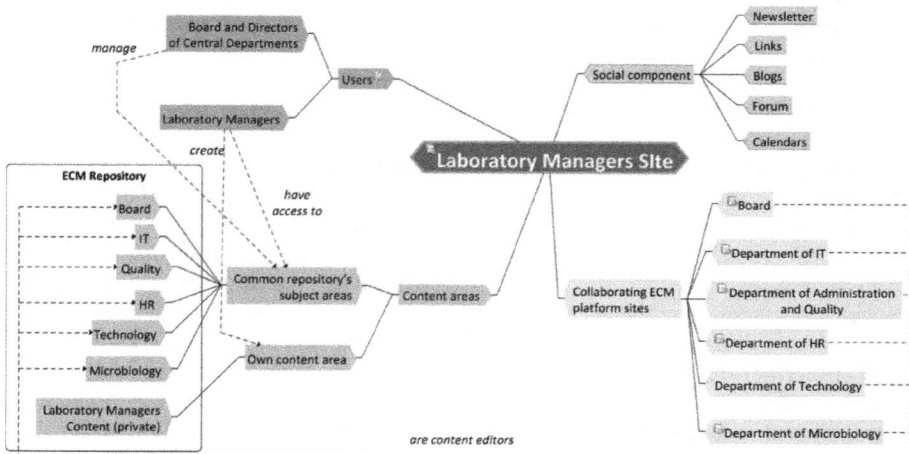

Figure 5.
Content map of laboratory managers site (mind maps notation).

and practical experience confirm that most of the content processes modeled are ordered workflows unlike ad hoc processes, which also appeared in the project. Since there are certain differences in understanding and modeling between the two types, each of them constitutes a separate ECM3 subperspective. Because of the fact workflows are prevailing and the chapter's length is limited, the ad hoc processes subperspective will be presented in the author's future articles.

Workflow processes have a defined path (compliant with organization's rules) including alternative and parallel executions. Ordering workflow processes present in the ECM area is a consequence of organizational rules, which determine what the correspondence flow, invoice authorization, or quality document preparation should look like. The rules are described in official regulations and procedures, accepted by the board and to be obeyed by every employee.

Workflow is based on roles resulting from the company's organizational structure. Assigning employees and groups of them to particular process activities realization occurs where the two perspectives meet. We may say that process described in this way becomes the basis to be implemented in ECM platform process engine. Today, selecting process modeling tools is much easier as in 2004, Object Management Group (OMG) published the first standard covering the area—Business Process Model and Notation (BPMN) [19]. When it comes to ECM platform implementation, the standard's (currently v. 2.0) superiority manifests in the fact that process engines also make use of graphic notations, mostly BPMN. Using XML format like Business Process Execution Language (BPEL) for transferring models between various tools by other developers—CASE tools and the abovementioned process engines—is yet another advantage of the standard. The notation's foundations are easy to learn and comprehend by the model's receivers. A few-minute-long introduction to its principles and elements' meaning is enough for them to actively participate in the analytical team. BPMN has also another, extended "implementation" version; being much more complex and consisting of a number of notation elements, it is rarely used at the analytical stage.

BPMN's swimlines are an extremely important concept in content workflow modeling. In large organizations, content workflow models do not consist of many activities or diverse paths (e.g., invoice circulation process is made up of registration, description, approval, and booking). The main focus there is to model who the activities will be performed by depending on the document's type or its target location.

BPMN is not devoid of disadvantages. As it is supposed to present the workflow and communication between the process' participants, it does not show more detailed information on the documents or document sets being processed. The project used the recommendations offered in [29] and the author's own data objects naming convention.

5.3 Organizational structure perspective

Organizational structure primarily "links organizational units and positions within an organization" [30]. When considering its significance in content workflows, we need to note its function in management theory. The organizational structure analysis performed by Stabryła [31] distinguishes its three outstanding functions vital to content workflow: designating the assignment of work within the system, placing the processes across time (harmonization) and space (shows where the processes are realized), and determining resources (informational and technical). Practical experience shows that proper understanding of the functions is crucial to modeling not only organizational structure but also other ECM3 methodology perspectives. Organizational structure provides content workflow with individual activity performers (via roles which very often directly relate to positions, e.g., Lab Manager or professional superior). Roles also correspond to the employees' functions resulting from the organizational structure, e.g., warehouse-man role indicates employee(s) of the Warehousing Department. Organizational structure is not only used in the processes but also in the content perspective when building ECM repository's layout, creating content access mechanism or platform sites' structure. The project execution has demonstrated that because of its signifi-cance, organizational structure perspective should be the foundation for model building in an organization implementing ECM.

Selecting suitable modeling tool is not easy as the perspective is relatively young and underestimated. The process included a comparison of ARIS, BPMS, EA, and OrgChart in the context of organizational structure and its results were presented in the author's article [16]. The tool picked was the oldest and most popular business notation—OrgChart [32]. OrgChart is an extremely simple notation—it consists of one notation element (denoting organizational unit or post) and single relation denoting subjection. It's simplicity, accessibility, and popularity, which make it so well received by business users, become limitations for analysts. The main one is the lack of clear distinction between organizational unit's artifacts: cell, post, person, and role. Another one is problem with mapping a large organization consisting of up to few hundred organizational units. In order to eliminate these restraints, stereotyping and decomposition were proposed. Stereotyping means the ability to divide notation elements into types (marked with <<..>> symbol known from UML). Decomposition consists in dividing a wide organizational structure into levels which ultimately provides us with a multilevel model equipped with a level navigation mechanism.

Figure 6 presents a single diagnostic lab with its organizational cells, posts, persons, and roles. Stereotyping mechanism was used. The roles mentioned in the diagram will be part of the medical procedure document flow.

5.4 Locational structure perspective

ECM platforms are popular in organizations searching for uniform, central, and common access content storage and processing space. Problems appear for

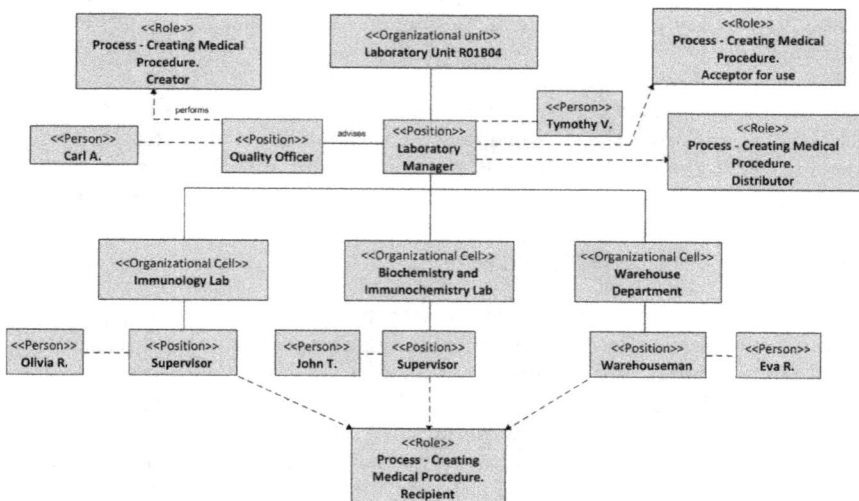

Figure 6.
Single laboratory structure (OrgChart notation).

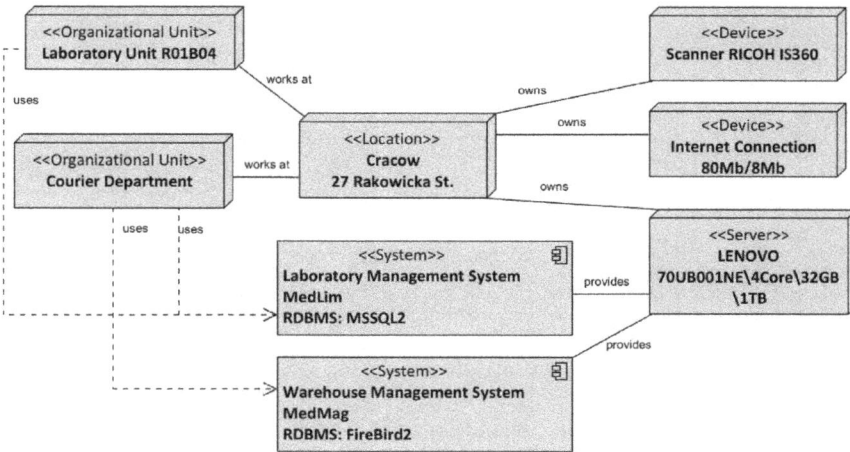

Figure 7.
Single place of document inflow (locational diagram notation).

organizations consisting of an extensive structure of physical locations where their business is run. The company subject to this chapter is a multibranch organization spread across the whole country. Switching from traditional physical document circulation to electronic one required detailed planning of a countrywide locations network. Subsequently, we had to answer the question to which locations the documents were delivered (and in what form) and which locations they were sent from, taking into account both internal and external receivers. Next step consisted in defining the IT equipment requirements for the locations (scanners, barcode scanners, printers, etc.) as well as infrastructure and software, which would be used in each of the locations by employees realizing their tasks on ECM platform. One should note that locations are not identical with organizational units (it occurs occasionally in smaller organizations). When planning a locational structure, we have to consider which organizational units use individual locations.

To date IS analysis and design methodologies have been practically devoid of the locational structure perspective. Some of its elements could be found in tools like BMPS or ARIS. Detailed comparison has been presented in one of the author's papers [16]. Since there were no ready tools dedicated to handle all the requirements, an attempt was made to extend one of the UML diagrams—deployment diagram. The diagram represents distribution of physical and software components (node elements) and their mutual relations [22]. The notation was extended with locational and organizational unit nodes support but the principles for the diagram's creation remained unchanged (named locational diagram). **Figure 7** presents a single location with two organizational units. The location is prepared to work on an ECM platform (is equipped with the right hardware, software, and connections). Decomposition can be used to build a collective locations network.

6. Conclusion

The chapter presents the second stage of the research whose aim was to create an integrated and comprehensive modeling methodology dedicated to organization preparing for ECM platform implementation, and specifically the process of analytical tool selection for key tactical perspectives on enterprise defined in the ECM3

Perspective	Subperspective	Recommended modeling tools
Content	Unstructured content	XML, ERD, UML class diagram
	Structured content	ERD, UML class diagram
	ECM platform map	Mind maps diagram
Processes (content workflow)	Workflow	BPMN
	Work group ad hoc processes	BPMN, CMMN
Organizational structure		OrgChart (including the author's modifications)
Locational structure		Locational diagram (the author's proposition)

Table 1.
A set of selected perspectives and ECM3 methodology tools.

methodology. ECM3's main perspectives are content, process (content workflow), organizational structure, locational structure, business rules, and IT environment. The chapter describes tools for the first four. An ordered list of the perspectives, subperspectives, and recommended tools is shown in **Table 1**.

The tools selected meet two core criteria—open accessibility and significant comprehensibility for non-IT business users participating in the platform's implementation. Fulfillment of the last criterion was verified in the project subject to this chapter—ECM platform implementation in a medical multibranch enterprise. All of the presented tools were demonstrated, tested, and enhanced by an analytical team which the author was a member of. Without problem reporting, criticism and numerous valuable ideas from the people cooperating with the author the ECM3 methodology's development would not be possible.

The author's next short-term research plans will focus on the description of tool selection for the two remaining ECM3 perspectives: business rules and IT environment. Next, more complex stages of ECM3 methodology development will be researched: analytical procedure, rules for analytical team member selection, and supporting IT tools. ECM3 is going to evolve for two reasons. First, the whole ECM domain is going to evolve—new technologies will be involved, new strategies created, completely new areas for the abovementioned elements' use will appear. Second, people facing the task of ECM tools implementation in an organization will have a much better knowledge and deeper experience in the subject area—the author invites all of them to cooperate.

Acknowledgements

I would like to thank my Alma Mater, Cracow University of Economics, for sponsoring this publication. The research has been financed by the funds granted to the Faculty of Management, within the subsidy for maintaining research potential.

I would also like to thank the board of directors and the numerous employees of the case study company for their kindness, knowledge, and experience sharing and their consent to the case study results presentation.

Author details

Jan Trąbka
Department of Computer Science, Cracow University of Economics, Cracow,
Poland

*Address all correspondence to: jan.trabka@uek.krakow.pl

IntechOpen

References

[1] Gantz J, Reiznel D. The Digital Universe in 2020: Big Data, Bigger Digital Shadows, and Biggest Growth in the Far East. 2012. Available from: http://www.emc.com/collateral/analyst-reports/idc-the-digital-universe-in-2020.pdf [Accessed: Jun 12, 2018]

[2] Mancini J. The Emperor's New Clothes: The Current State of Information Management Compliance. 2004. Available from: http://www.tasmea.com/pdf/whitepapers/Industry_Watch_Compliance.pdf [Accessed: May 20, 2018]

[3] Association for Information and Image Management. What is Enterprise Content Management. 2018. Available from: http://www.aiim.org/What-is-ECM-Enterprise-Content-Management [Accessed: Jun 5, 2018]

[4] Research and Markets. Global ERP Software Market Analysis & Trends—Industry Forecast to 2025. 2017. Available from: https://www.researchandmarkets.com/reports/4399984/global-erp-software-market-analysis-and-trends. [Accessed: 04-06-2018]

[5] Research and Markets. Global Enterprise Content Management (ECM) Market 2018-2022. 2018. Available from: https://www.researchandmarkets.com/research/wrsm97/global_enterprise?w=5. [Accessed: 10-06-2018]

[6] Simons A, vom Brocke J. Enterprise content management in information systems research. In: vom Brocke J, Simons A, editors. Enterprise Content Management in Information Systems Research—Foundations, Methods and Cases. Berlin: Springer-Verlag; 2014

[7] Trąbka J. A proposal for an ECM systems modeling method—Defining tactical perspective—Lesson learnt

from a case study. In: Wrycza S, Maślankowski J, editors. Information Systems: Research, Development, Applications, Education. Berlin: Springer; 2017. pp. 136-151

[8] Trąbka J. Enterprise content management platforms: Concept update, role in organization and main technologies. In: Pańkowska M, Palonka J, Sroka H, editors. Ambient Technology and Creativity Support Systems. Katowice: University of Economics in Katowice; 2013. pp. 192-205

[9] Koehler-Kruener H, Chin K, Hob K. Magic Quadrant for ECM 2015. Gartner: Stamford; 2015

[10] Hobert K, Tay G, Mariano J. Magic Quadrant for ECM 2016. Gartner: Stamford; 2016

[11] Tyrväinen P, Päivärinta T, Salminen A, Iivari J. Characterizing the evolving research on enterprise content management. European Journal of Information Systems. 2006;**15**(6):627-634

[12] Rockley A, Cooper C. Managing Enterprise Content. A Unified Content Strategy. Second Edition. Berkeley: New Riders; 2012

[13] Peffers K, Tuunanen T, Rothenberger M, Chatterjee S. A design science research methodology for information systems research. Journal of Management Information Systems. 2007;**24**(3):45-78

[14] Markus M, Majchrzak A, Gasser L. A design theory for systems that support emergent knowledge processes. MIS Quarterly. 2002;**26**(3):179-212

[15] Reeves T, Herrington J, Oliver R. Design research: A socially responsible approach to instructional technology research in higher education. Journal

of Computing in Higher Education, 2005;**16**(2):96-115

[16] Trąbka J. Modeling organizational and locational structure in enterprise content management system adoptions: Experience from a large polish medical. Information Systems Management. 2017;**34**(4):359-377

[17] Hevner R, March S, Park J, Ram S. Design science in information system research. MIS Quarterly. 2004;**28**(1):75-105

[18] Yourdon E. Modern Structured Analysis. New York: Prentice Hall; 1988

[19] Object Management Group. About BPMN. 2011. Available from: https://www.omg.org/spec/BPMN/2.0/About-BPMN/. [Accessed: Jun 5, 2018]

[20] Object Management Group. About the Unified Modeling Language Specification Version 2.0. 2005. Available from: https://www.omg.org/spec/UML/2.0/About-UML/. [Accessed: May 10, 2018]

[21] Wrycza S, Marcinkowski B, Wyrzykowski K. Język UML 2.0 w modelowaniu systemów informatycznych (UML 2.0 in Modeling Information Systems). Helion: Gliwice; 2005

[22] Coronel C, Moris S. Database Systems: Design, Implementation, & Management. 13th ed. Boston: Cengage; 2017

[23] Bia A, Gomez J. UML for document modeling: Designing document structures for massive and systematic production of XML-based web contents. In: Briand L, Williams C, editors. Model Driven Engineering Languages and Systems. Lecture Notes in Computer Science. Berlin, Heidelberg: Springer; 2005. pp. 648-658

[24] Buzan T, Buzan N. The Mind Map Book: How to Use Radiant Thinking to Maximize Your Brain's Untapped Potential. Plume: New York City; 1996

[25] Żbikowska K. Mapy myśli w biznesie. Jak twórczo i efektywnie osiągać cele za pomocą mind mappingu. Helion: Gliwice; 2012

[26] Deer J. Content Mapping [Internet]. 2012. Available from: https://www.webpagefx.com/blog/web-design/content-mapping/ [Accessed: Feb 22, 2018]

[27] Visual Paradigm. Visual Paradigm Site. 2016. Available from: http://www.visual-paradigm.com/ [Accessed: Dec 12, 2016]

[28] Gilbert M, Shegda K, Chin K, Koehler-Kruener H. Magic Quadrant for ECM 2014. Gartner: Stamford; 2014

[29] Gawin B, Marcinkowski B. Symulacja procesów biznesowych. Standardy BPMS i BPMN w praktyce (Simulating business process. BPMS and BPMN standards in practice). Helion: Gliwice; 2013

[30] Nelson DL, Quick JC. Understanding Organizational Behavior. A Multimedia Approach. Ohio: South Western; 2002

[31] Stabryła A. Doskonalenie struktur organizacyjnych przedsiębiorstw w gospodarce opartej na wiedzy (Improving the Enterprise Organizational Structure in the Knowledge Economy). C.H. Beck: Warsaw; 2009

[32] Haskell A, Breaznell J. Graphic Charts in Business: How to Make and Use Them. New York: Codex Book Company; 1922

Section 3

Simulation Theory

Chapter 4

Petri Net Models Optimized for Simulation

Juan-Ignacio Latorre-Biel and Emilio Jiménez-Macías

Abstract

Petri nets and simulation are a modeling paradigm and a tool, respectively, which may be successfully combined for diverse applications, such as performance evaluation, decision support, or training on complex systems. Simulation may require significant computer resources; hence, in this chapter, two Petri net-based formalisms are analyzed for profiting from their respective advantages for modeling, simulation, and decision-making support: a set of alternative Petri nets and a compound Petri net. These formalisms, as well as the transformation algorithms between them, are detailed and an illustrative example is provided. Among the main advantages of these formalisms, their intuitive application for modeling discrete event systems in the process of being designed, as well as the compactness that may present the resulting model, in the case of a compound Petri net, leading to efficient decision making, can be mentioned.

Keywords: alternative Petri nets, compound Petri nets, parametric Petri nets, modeling and simulation, decision support systems

1. Introduction

Simulation can be considered as a tool able to mimic, in an approximated way, some of the properties and the behavior of a certain system. This system can be real or imaginary; hence, simulation can imply a significant saving of money and time, when applied to large and expensive systems, such as manufacturing facilities or road networks, and when implemented to systems that do not exist, such as in the design of products or the development of computer games. The purposes for the application of simulation can be to improve the knowledge of a certain system, to train and educate, to develop games, or to test certain features of systems, such as safety issues. However, the main application field of simulation is decision making. In this context, simulation allows knowing in advance the effects of making certain decisions on a system of interest. As an outcome of a series of simulations, testing different decisions, it is possible to select the best solution or to provide to a human decision maker some information on the effects of certain decisions and how these effects are compatible with the objectives of the decision process. This chapter will focus mainly on the simulation applied to the broad field of decision-making support.

1.1 Decision support systems

Our present technological civilization offers many opportunities for the application of decision support systems. Decision making is a demanding task in systems that show a complex behavior, such as manufacturing systems, supply chains, hospitals, educative institutions, communication networks, just to give a few examples.

Decisions made by experts, who base their choices on their intuition and experience, present evident limitations, since these professionals are scarce resources and expensive to hire. Additionally, human decision makers may be influenced by personal affinities and prejudices and they might tend to simplify reality, limiting the number of feasible solutions to be considered, as well as to skip information that might be relevant in the decision problem.

One solution to the challenge of decision making in complex systems can be the development of a decision support system and its application to solve a specific problem [1]. Different types of decision support systems can be developed for a variety of complex systems and decision problems. A particular kind of methodology for the construction of such support systems is based on the development of a model of the complex system of interest. This model can be analyzed to deduce some properties that may be useful to understand the system itself, as well as to improve it according to the objectives of the decision makers.

1.2 Petri nets in decision support systems

Many complex systems of technological, financial, and social interest can be considered as discrete event systems [2]. The development of a quantitative model of a discrete event system requires the use of a certain formal language to describe it. Petri nets have proven to be very suitable for modeling complex discrete event systems. A large amount of theoretical results and applications of this formalism are available in the scientific literature [3–5].

Petri nets, as a formal language, have been used extensively to model successfully complex discrete event systems in a broad range of application areas: industrial manufacturing, food industry, transportation systems, road networks, railway networks, communication networks, ports, airports, etc.

A Petri net model of a discrete event system can be considered as a mathematical description of this system. This description contains numbers that quantify certain features of the original system. Depending on the class of Petri net, considered to represent the model of the system, the roles these numbers may play are more or less diverse. For example, an autonomous generalized Petri net would present numbers that represent the initial marking of the places of the net, as well as the weight of every arc between places and transitions [6]. A timed Petri net would present numbers associated to the delay time of firing certain transitions once they are enabled. A prioritized Petri net may present numbers associated to the priority in firing any transition involved in effective conflicts. These are just some examples of the richness of the feasible meaning that a certain number in a Petri net model can show.

A decision problem, implying a Petri net model of a discrete event system, involves one or several decision variables, which are usually associated to one of the numbers of the mathematical description that constitutes the Petri net [7]. The objective of the decision process is to determine a value for every decision variable that meets the objectives of the decision makers and the additional constraints the problem might present [8]. According to this approach, the decision variables can be called parameters of the Petri net model and they might be the initial marking of certain places, weight of some arcs between nodes of the net, delay times associated to a given set of transitions, etc. [9].

The most common parameters of a Petri net, involved in a decision-making process, are associated to the initial marking of the net and to the weight of the arcs.

The weight of the arcs of a Petri net is ranked as elements of the so-called incidence matrices. It is known that the structure of the Petri net model, and hence the structure of the original system, is represented by means of the incidence matrices, or the weight of the arcs between nodes of the net. This structure is, somehow, the part of the model that remains unchanged, when the Petri net evolves.

Furthermore, the dynamics of the Petri net is described by the changing marking of the net, as a consequence of firing a sequence of transitions. In fact, it is said that the places, which hold the tokens of the marking, are the state variables of the discrete event system, and their values are the marking at a given frame in the evolution of the net.

As a consequence, a decision problem related to the operation of a system, such as specifying the number of resources a certain production in a manufacturing facility would require, is likely to involve Petri net with parameters in the initial marking of certain places [10]. These parameters can be called marking parameters. Moreover, a decision problem involving the design of a new system or a significant redesign of an existing one is probably related to a Petri net containing parameters in the incidence matrices, which can be called structural parameters [11]. The former is a relatively common problem in the scientific literature, while the latter is a much scarcer case. In fact, the design of a discrete event system is, commonly, a much more difficult problem than its mere operation. Not in vain, the design of a discrete event system can be carried out solving in parallel the problem of operating it, in order to obtain from the designed system its maximal "benefit."

1.3 Simulation as a tool for decision making

One group of methodologies to solve decision problems associated to Petri net models is based on simulation [12]. This approach has been successfully applied to a diversity of case studies described in the literature. Basically, the use of simulation in conjunction with a Petri net model may imply the following steps:

a. Select one solution to the decision problem. This step can be carried out by intuition, randomly, using a heuristic or metaheuristic algorithm, etc.

b. Assign values from the chosen solution to every parameter of the Petri net (decision variables).

c. Simulate the evolution of the Petri net until a certain stop criterion is met.

d. Analyze the outcome of the simulation process. This step can be developed by calculating a quality parameter that quantifies the degree of verification of the objectives of the decision maker by the tested solution.

e. Select and test another solution and compare the outcome of its simulation with the previously tested solutions.

f. When a certain stop criterion is met, finish the procedure.

Simulation is a very useful methodology for decision making in systems that cannot stop their operation for testing their performance after different decisions or these tests are too expensive or the feasible outcome is too risky to be carried out [13]. For example, this situation arises in the case of a manufacturing facility, where the change of the manufacturing strategy may present important implications for the survival of the company [3, 14]. Furthermore, simulation is even more important in the design of systems, since in the design process it is not always possible to test solutions in a system that does not exist yet.

The feasible solutions of a decision problem can be found in the solution space. This space might be huge, in particular when a combinatorial process can be used to build up solutions for the decision problem. This is the case when the structure of a solution contains the decision variables (parameters) of a Petri net and by combining in different ways the diverse values the decision variables can take; the solution space is constructed.

To be confident in making good decisions, the number of tested solutions should be large, when comparing it to the size of the solution space. However, testing one solution implies to carry out one simulation. However, simulation can consume a large amount of computer resources. Adding this fact to a huge solution space implies that, in general, it is not possible to analyze a significant percentage of the solutions contained in the solution space. As a consequence, it is crucial to use efficient search algorithms to select good solutions to be tested. Furthermore, it is very convenient to use efficient simulation methodologies to reduce the computer resources a simulation process requires [15].

This chapter is devoted to studying different approaches for modeling with Petri nets a system in the process of being designed, whose Petri net model contains at least one structural parameter. This analysis aims at providing modeling tools to improve the simulation of a Petri net, when compared with a classic approach. In particular, some of the advantages for simulation the presented formalisms would provide are:

a. Removal of redundant information in the model of the system, hence, reducing its size.

b. Feasibility of automatic solving of the decision problem, hence, testing a large number of solutions.

c. More efficient exploration of the solution space, hence focusing on the most promising regions to obtain good solutions.

Petri nets and their graphical and matrix-based representations are the topic of the second section of this chapter. This overview of some properties of the Petri nets will be applied in the following section.

In Section 1 of this chapter, it was shown how a decision problem could be stated to solve the design of a discrete event system. This kind of decision problem is usually related to the specification of the structure of the system in the process of being designed. One possibility to represent a model of a Petri net, whose structure is not completely defined, is to consider structural parameters or decision variables in the incidence matrices of the net. However, there are other different feasible representations of a discrete event system with a noncompletely specified structure, such as the set of alternative Petri nets, which is the topic of the third section of the chapter.

The description of a Petri net, whose structure is not known, because its design has not been completed or it is being modified, can also be done by means of parameters in its incidence matrices. This type of Petri net can be called parametric Petri net. Section 4 of this chapter devotes to the compound Petri nets, a particular type of parametric Petri net, which contains at least one structural parameter.

The following section describes and illustrates the transformation of a set of alternative Petri nets into a compound Petri net and vice versa. These transformation algorithms allow profiting from the advantages of the different formal languages at the diverse stages of the decision-making process.

The chapter ends with the conclusions and bibliographical references.

The main objective of this chapter is to show the application of Petri net models optimized for simulation in a decision support system. The adaptation of the Petri net models to these systems is based on the development of formal languages that profit from the characteristics of the discrete event systems and the decision support methodology to reduce the computational resources applied to decision support.

2. Petri nets

2.1 Graphical representation of a Petri net

Among the more outstanding characteristics of a Petri net model, it is possible to mention a double graphical and matrix-based representation. The former may show, in a very intuitive way, the components or subsystems of the discrete event system and how they relate. Additionally, the tokens, representing the marking of the Petri net, configure a distributed state of the system, which informs about the dynamics of the system.

On the contrary, the matrix-based representation is an appropriate description of the discrete event system to process the model in a computer, in order to develop a structural analysis or a performance evaluation [5]. Among the tools that can be used to study the structure and behavior of the system, simulation can be mentioned. Moreover, the structure of the Petri net model is also shown in this matrix-based representation, by means of the incidence matrices. Subsystems appear as boxes in the matrices, while their interrelations, in the form of transitions, are shown as columns of the incidence matrices.

These ideas are very useful for the development and application of Petri nets–based formalisms to represent appropriate models in the frame of decision-making processes.

In this section, some ideas on the graphical representation of a Petri net are stated [3].

Definition 1. Marked generalized Petri net

A marked generalized *Petri net* is a 5-tuple:

$$N = \langle P, T, \text{pre}, \text{post}, \mathbf{m}_0 \rangle. \tag{1}$$

where
P and T are disjoint, nonempty, finite sets of places and transitions, respectively.
Pre: $P \times T \to N$ is called the input or preincidence function.
Post: $T \times P \to N$ is called the output or postincidence function.
$\mathbf{m}_0$ is the initial marking of P and $\mathbf{m}_0 = (m_1, m_2, ..., m_n)^{\text{T}} \in \mathbf{N}^n$. The ith component of $\mathbf{m}_0$ is the marking of place $p_i \in P$.

□

The sets of places and transitions in addition to the input and output functions determine the structure of a Petri net, while the marking characterizes its dynamics.

A Petri net can be seen as a bipartite graph with oriented arcs, where the nodes can belong to a set of places or a set of transitions and the arcs relate to couples of nodes of different types. In other words, an arc cannot relate a place with another (or the same) place or a transition with another (or the same) transition. Additionally, an arc can be represented from a place to a transition or from a transition to a place. In both cases, there is a clear and different implication of the arc in the behavior of the Petri net model. In certain classes of Petri nets, generalized Petri nets, natural numbers are represented in conjunction with the arcs. These weights represent different things depending on the type of arc:

a. If the arc starts in a place and finishes in a transition, the weight of the arc presents two meanings. The first one is the number of tokens in the place that constitutes a necessary condition to enable the transition, previous step to firing it. The sufficient condition to enable the transition is that the number of tokens in all the input places of the transition is equal or greater to the weight of the arcs from the input places to the mentioned transition. The second meaning of one of these input arcs is the number of tokens that are removed from the place, when the transition fires.

b. If the arc starts in a transition and finishes in a place, the weight of the arc corresponds to the number of tokens added to the output place, once the transition is fired.

Tokens may flow from one or several places to other ones through fired transitions. This flow represents the evolution of the Petri net model by means of the variation of the state of the model (represented by means of the Petri net marking).

The input and output functions can be represented in a matrix-based way by means of the so-called input and output incidence matrices $W-$ and $W+$. These matrices contain the weight of the arcs from places to transitions and from transitions to places, respectively. Each row is associated to a given place of the Petri net and each column to a certain transition.

2.2 Matrix-based representation of a Petri net

The input incidence matrix, W^+, ranks the weight of the arcs from places to transitions. The element of the matrix placed in the ith row and jth transition, w_{ij}^+, corresponds to the weight of the arc that starts in the jth place and finishes in the ith transition. It is a natural deduction that interchanging the name (number) between two places or two transitions has two implications:

a. The structure and behavior of the Petri net do not change, since the graphical representation of the Petri net remains the same, as well as the initial marking and other features of the net.

b. The two rows (columns) associated to the places (transitions) that have interchanged the names are swapped, thus leading to a different incidence matrix.

c. Swapping rows or columns of the incidence matrices does not modify the structure or the behavior of the Petri net.

As it has been seen, the input incidence matrix represents the number of tokens that the firing of a transition removes from each input place.

The output incidence matrix is composed of the weight of the arcs from transitions to places. The element of the matrix that is located in the ith row and jth column, w_{ij}^-, consists of the weight of the arc beginning in the jth transition and finishing in the ith place. This output incidence matrix represents the number of tokens that the firing of each transition adds to each output place.

From the point of view of the ith place, p_i, the number of tokens that remain after the firing of the jth transition, t_j, is the balance between the following:

a. The weight of the arc that starts in the jth transition and ends in the ith place, w_{ij}^+. This number adds w_{ij}^+ tokens to the place p_i.

b. The weight of the arc that starts in the ith place and ends in the jth transition, w_{ij}^-. This number subtracts w_{ij}^- tokens to the place p_i.

This balance can be represented as $w_{ij}^+ - w_{ij}^-$. As a consequence, a single incidence matrix can be built up from the input and output incidence matrices:

$$W = W^+ - W^-. \tag{2}$$

From the graphical representation of the Petri net or from the input and output incidence matrix, it is possible to obtain this single incidence matrix W. However, the reconstruction of the original Petri net (described by its graphical representation or by the input and output incidence matrices) is not possible in the case when at least one of the element of the incidence matrix $w_{ij} = w_{ij}^+ - w_{ij}^-$ is obtained by the subtraction of two elements of the input and output incidence matrices different to zero: $w_{ij}^+ \neq 0$ and $w_{ij}^- \neq 0$. This situation corresponds to a Petri net, where at least one transition is, both, input and output transition of a given place.

A Petri net not presenting any transition that is simultaneously input and output transition of the same place is called pure Petri net. The simulation of a Petri net requires the calculation of a sequence of markings (states) that are allowed by the Petri net structure, the initial marking, and other additional restrictions that might arise (such as delay times, priorities, etc.).

3. Set of alternative Petri nets

3.1 Definition and properties

One classic and usually intuitive way to represent a system with a noncompletely specified structure is a set of alternative Petri nets [16]. This approach arises naturally, when considering a discrete event system in the process of being designed as a Petri net with alternative structural configurations [17].

The classic approach, when a discrete event system is to be designed, or, more generally, its structure is to be specified, consists of selecting (manually) a small set of alternative structures to be tested as final solutions for the decision problem.

This modeling strategy may lead to a lack of generality by focusing on a reduced set of alternative structural configurations. However, it is intuitive, simple to apply, and, in general, its analysis requires a reduced amount of computer resources.

Basically, a set of alternative Petri nets contains exclusive models for a certain discrete event system presenting different static structures. Any pair of nets belonging to such a set verifies the following property, which guarantees the exclusiveness between the feasible models for the original discrete event system.

Definition 2. Mutually exclusive evolution

Given two Petri nets R and R', they are said to have mutually exclusive evolutions if they verify:

i. If $\mathbf{m}(R) \neq \mathbf{m_0}(R) \Rightarrow \mathbf{m}(R') = \mathbf{m_0}(R')$.

ii. If $\mathbf{m}(R') \neq \mathbf{m_0}(R) \Rightarrow \mathbf{m}(R) = \mathbf{m_0}(R)$.

☐

In addition to the previous property, any couple of Petri nets should meet an additional constraint to be considered as alternative Petri nets.

Definition 3. Pair of alternative Petri nets

Given two Petri nets R and R', they are said to be alternative Petri nets if they verify:

i. R and R' have mutually exclusive evolutions.

ii. $\mathbf{W}(R) \neq \mathbf{W}(R')$, where $\mathbf{W}(R) \neq \mathbf{W}(R')$ are the incidence matrices of R and R', respectively.

☐

Definition 4. Set of alternative Petri nets

Given a set of Petri nets $S_R = \{R_1, ..., R_n\}$, S_R is said to be a set of alternative Petri nets if it verifies:

i. $n > 1$.

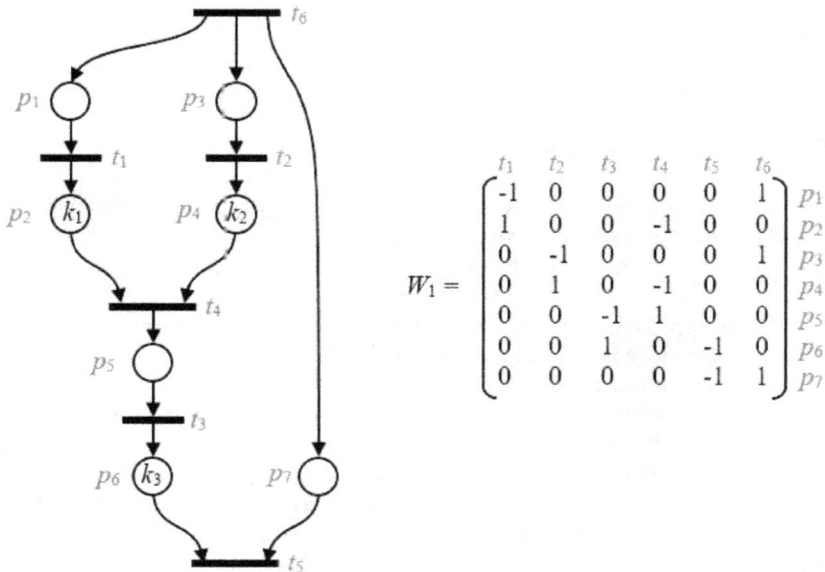

$$
W_1 = \begin{array}{c} \\ \\ \\ \\ \\ \\ \\ \end{array}
\begin{array}{cccccc}
t_1 & t_2 & t_3 & t_4 & t_5 & t_6 \\
\left[\begin{array}{cccccc}
-1 & 0 & 0 & 0 & 0 & 1 \\
1 & 0 & 0 & -1 & 0 & 0 \\
0 & -1 & 0 & 0 & 0 & 1 \\
0 & 1 & 0 & -1 & 0 & 0 \\
0 & 0 & -1 & 1 & 0 & 0 \\
0 & 0 & 1 & 0 & -1 & 0 \\
0 & 0 & 0 & 0 & -1 & 1
\end{array}\right] & \begin{array}{c} p_1 \\ p_2 \\ p_3 \\ p_4 \\ p_5 \\ p_6 \\ p_7 \end{array}
\end{array}
$$

Figure 1.
Manufacturing line under a push strategy.

ii. $\forall\, i, j \in \mathbf{N}$, such that $i \neq j$ and $1 \leq i, j \leq n$, then R_i and R_j are a pair of alternative Petri nets.

$\square$

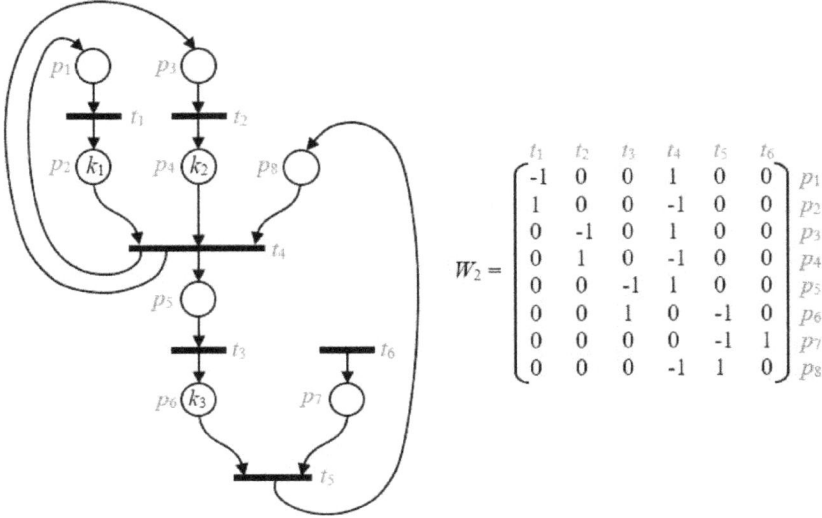

$$W_2 = \begin{array}{c} \begin{array}{cccccc} t_1 & t_2 & t_3 & t_4 & t_5 & t_6 \end{array} \\ \left[\begin{array}{cccccc} -1 & 0 & 0 & 1 & 0 & 0 \\ 1 & 0 & 0 & -1 & 0 & 0 \\ 0 & -1 & 0 & 1 & 0 & 0 \\ 0 & 1 & 0 & -1 & 0 & 0 \\ 0 & 0 & -1 & 1 & 0 & 0 \\ 0 & 0 & 1 & 0 & -1 & 0 \\ 0 & 0 & 0 & 0 & -1 & 1 \\ 0 & 0 & 0 & -1 & 1 & 0 \end{array} \right] \begin{array}{c} p_1 \\ p_2 \\ p_3 \\ p_4 \\ p_5 \\ p_6 \\ p_7 \\ p_8 \end{array} \end{array}$$

Figure 2.
Manufacturing line under an SKCS strategy.

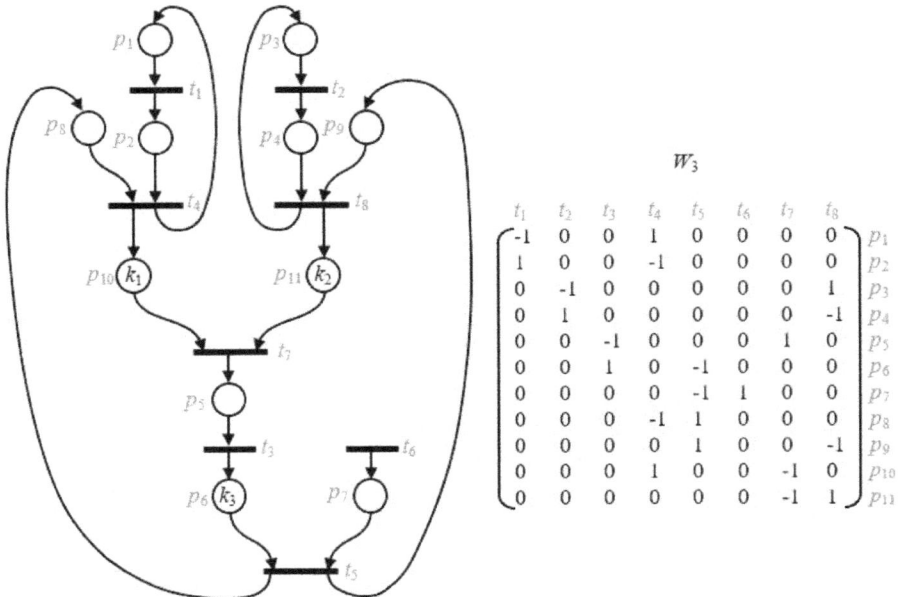

$$W_3$$

$$\begin{array}{c} \begin{array}{cccccccc} t_1 & t_2 & t_3 & t_4 & t_5 & t_6 & t_7 & t_8 \end{array} \\ \left[\begin{array}{cccccccc} -1 & 0 & 0 & 1 & 0 & 0 & 0 & 0 \\ 1 & 0 & 0 & -1 & 0 & 0 & 0 & 0 \\ 0 & -1 & 0 & 0 & 0 & 0 & 0 & 1 \\ 0 & 1 & 0 & 0 & 0 & 0 & 0 & -1 \\ 0 & 0 & -1 & 0 & 0 & 0 & 1 & 0 \\ 0 & 0 & 1 & 0 & -1 & 0 & 0 & 0 \\ 0 & 0 & 0 & 0 & -1 & 1 & 0 & 0 \\ 0 & 0 & 0 & -1 & 1 & 0 & 0 & 0 \\ 0 & 0 & 0 & 0 & 1 & 0 & 0 & -1 \\ 0 & 0 & 0 & 1 & 0 & 0 & -1 & 0 \\ 0 & 0 & 0 & 0 & 0 & 0 & -1 & 1 \end{array} \right] \begin{array}{c} p_1 \\ p_2 \\ p_3 \\ p_4 \\ p_5 \\ p_6 \\ p_7 \\ p_8 \\ p_9 \\ p_{10} \\ p_{11} \end{array} \end{array}$$

Figure 3.
Manufacturing line under an IKCS strategy.

3.2 Examples

In order to illustrate the concept of set of alternative Petri nets, an example from [18] is shown. In this example, different manufacturing strategies are shown for their application to a manufacturing line composed of two manufacturing stages followed by an assembly stage. **Figure 1** represents a basic pull control strategy, named base sock control system (BSCS). **Figure 2** shows a simultaneous Kanban control system (SKCS) and **Figure 3** depicts an independent Kanban control system (IKCS). All these figures contain a graphical and a matrix-based representation of the Petri net models. More examples of sets of alternative Petri nets can be found in [19, 20].

4. Compound Petri net/parametric Petri net

4.1 Definition and features

In this section, a compound Petri net is defined as a parametric Petri net that presents structural parameters [20]. Additionally, the equivalence between alternative Petri nets and a compound Petri net is analyzed. Furthermore, transformation algorithms are provided and an illustrative example of application is detailed.

As it has already been mentioned, a compound Petri net can be seen as a parametric Petri net with structural parameters. These are parameters in the incidence matrices or, what is the same, in the weight of some of the arcs of the net.

Definition 5. Compound Petri net

A compound Petri net is a 7-tuple $R^c = \langle P, T, \text{pre}, \text{post}, \mathbf{m_0}, S_\alpha, S_{val\alpha} \rangle$, where

i. S_α is the set of parameters of R^c.

ii. $S_{val\alpha}$ is the feasible combination of values for the parameters.

iii. $\exists\, S_{stra} \subseteq S_\alpha$, a set of structural parameters of R^c, such that $S_{stra} \neq \emptyset$, that is, a compound Petri net should contain at least one structural parameter.

$\square$

An example of a compound Petri net can be seen in **Figures 6** and 7. In the first of these figures, the incidence matrix is shown. The structural parameters have been represented by means of the symbol α and an ordinal subindex. In this example, the set of structural parameters S_{stra} coincides with the set of parameters S_α. These sets have been detailed in **Figure 6**.

Additionally, the set of feasible combinations of values for the parameters of the Petri net, $S_{val\alpha}$, can be found in this same figure. This important set should be given as a part of the Petri net model, in addition to the incidence matrices or the graphical representation of the net, since it provides the constraints that the values of the parameters should meet.

From this set, it is possible to determine the sets of feasible values for each one of the parameters of the Petri net. It is important to notice that the opposite statement is not true. In effect, given the set of feasible values for the different parameters of the Petri net:

$$S_{val\alpha 1} = \{0, 1, 1\}; S_{val\alpha 2} = \{1, 0, 0\}; S_{val\alpha 3} = \{0, 1, 0\}$$

$$S_{val\alpha 4} = \{1, 0, 0\}; S_{val\alpha 5} = \{0, 0, 1\}; S_{val\alpha 6} = \{1, 1, 0\}$$

$$S_{val\alpha 7} = \{0, 0, 1\}; S_{val\alpha 8} = \{1, 1, 0\}; S_{val\alpha 9} = \{0, 0, 1\}$$

$$S_{val\alpha 10} = \{0, 1, 1\}; S_{val\alpha 11} = \{0, 1, 1\}; S_{val\alpha 12} = \{0, 0, 1\}$$

$$S_{val\alpha 13} = \{0, 0, 1\}; S_{val\alpha 14} = \{0, 0, 1\}; S_{val\alpha 15} = \{0, 0, 1\}$$

$$S_{val\alpha 16} = \{0, 0, 1\}; S_{val\alpha 17} = \{0, 0, 1\}$$

It is not possible to obtain from them the set of feasible combinations of values for the parameters of the Petri net, $S_{val\alpha}$, since not all the combinations of values for each parameter is allowed. For example, even though α_1 and α_2 can take both 0 and 1 as feasible values, only the combinations $(\alpha_1, \alpha_2) \in \{(0, 1), (1, 0)\}$ are allowed but the combinations $(\alpha_1, \alpha_2) \notin \{(0, 0), (1, 1)\}$ are forbidden, since they do not take part in the Petri net intended as model of the original discrete event system.

4.2 Advantages and drawbacks

A compound Petri net presents a series of advantages, when compared to a set of alternative Petri nets, as model for a discrete event system with a structure that has not been completely designed yet:

(a.1) Compact model: if some alternative structural configurations present strong similarities, a compound Petri net as a metamodel representing all these configurations might imply a reduced set of structural parameters and the removal of a large amount of shared data. As a consequence, the resulting compound Petri net might present a size, which has been considerably reduced, when compared to an equivalent set of alternative Petri nets. In certain cases and applications, a more compact model may lead to faster computer processing of the model and, hence, faster decision-making support.

(a.2) Unified solution space: all the parameters of the Petri net are variable decisions, that is, components of a solution of a decision problem. The feasible combination of values for these parameters configures the solution space. There is no particular difference between structural parameters and other type of parameters of the Petri net, regarding the composition of a solution of the decision problem. As a consequence, a search for promising solutions is simplified and the search process itself can be performed more efficiently, since it can focus in the most promising regions of the solution space.

(a.3) Better understanding of the original discrete event system: a compound Petri net might point out the common structure in all the different feasible structures for the discrete event system, as well as constrain the differences in the structural parameters of the Petri net. This fact might enhance the knowledge of the system.

(a.4) Intuitive modeling: in case of a discrete event system in the process of being designed, the alternative structures that can be considered for the final model can be very similar. It is possible to think of a range of machines provided by the same supplier, which are essentially the same but presenting specific differences. It might be possible to develop a single model for all the machines, describing the common features of all of them. Then, this single model can be particularized for every different machine by representing with parameters their specific characteristics.

Despite these advantages, a compound Petri net may present certain drawbacks, when compared to a set of alternative Petri nets for describing a model of a discrete event system. In fact, depending on the real discrete event system to be modeled by Petri nets, some of the mentioned advantages can be considered as drawbacks of the compound Petri nets if a set of alternative Petri nets is more suitable to fulfill the needs of the decision makers.

(b.1) Novel approach: it is not difficult to find, in the scientific literature, sets of alternative Petri nets as feasible models for discrete event systems, even though they might not be referred by this name. Analyzing a small set of alternative Petri nets might be easier than analyzing a compound Petri net due to the larger availability of theoretical results that can be applied to the former, as well as due to the existence of efficient tools for simulation and performance evaluation, which are much more scarce for parametric Petri nets than for a set of alternative Petri nets.

(b.2) Nonintuitive modeling: this feature can be an advantage or a disadvantage of a set of alternative Petri nets, depending on the particular case study. In the case where the alternative structural configurations for the Petri net lead to very different incidence matrices, developing the model of the discrete event system may be much more difficult if the formalism of the compound Petri nets is used in the case where each structural configuration is modeled separately. This last approach produces a set of alternative Petri nets.

The next section will focus on the transformation algorithms between a set of alternative Petri nets and a compound Petri net. These algorithms allow transforming the formal language that describes the model of a system. However, the structure and dynamics of the model itself remain unchanged. These transformation algorithms allow profiting from the advantages of both, compound Petri nets and a set of alternative Petri nets, since certain stages of problem solving can be developed using one of the formalisms, while the other stages may be carried out describing the system with another formalism.

4.3 Transformation algorithms

4.3.1 Transformation of a set of alternative Petri nets into a compound Petri net

This section provides a sequence of steps to transform the formalism in which a model is represented, from a compound Petri net to a set of alternative Petri nets [21]. The application of this algorithm may allow the modeler to profit from the advantages of both formalisms in different stages of the process in which he or she is involved (e.g., a decision-making problem).

4.3.1.1 Step 1: development of a set of alternative Petri nets

This first step consists of building up a set of alternative Petri nets as feasible models of a discrete event system. As it has been explained in the previous section, in some cases, modeling a discrete event system by a set of alternative Petri nets can be a very intuitive process.

In **Figures 1–3**, three alternative Petri nets for a manufacturing line can be found. In each one of the mentioned figures, both the graphical representation and the incidence matrix of one of the alternative Petri nets are given. This set of alternative Petri nets is transformed in this section into a single compound Petri net.

4.3.1.2 Step 2: equaling the dimensions of the incidence matrices

In order to merge the three alternative Petri nets into one single compound Petri net requires having the same number of places and transitions in each case.

The first alternative Petri net presents 7 places and 6 transitions, the second, 8 places and 6 transitions, while the last one contains 11 places and 8 transitions. The variation of size of the alternative Petri nets should be made without changing the structure or the behavior of the nets. It is not always possible to reduce the size of a Petri net without modifying the structure or behavior. However, it is always possible to increase the size of a Petri net meeting these conditions by adding isolated places and/or transitions. An isolated place or transition does not present any input or output arc and, hence, it cannot participate in the dynamics of the Petri net and, of course, it cannot modify the behavior of the net.

The minimal size of the Petri nets, modified by adding places and/or transitions, is the size of the large alternative Petri net: 11 places and 8 transitions. As a consequence, four isolated places and two isolated transitions are added to the first alternative Petri net. Moreover, three places and two transitions are added to the second alternative Petri net. The third alternative Petri net remains unchanged. The incidence of the incorporation of isolated places and transitions to a Petri net in the incidence matrix is the addition of rows (one for each new place) and columns (one per new transition) of zeros. **Figure 4** shows partially the modified incidence matrices.

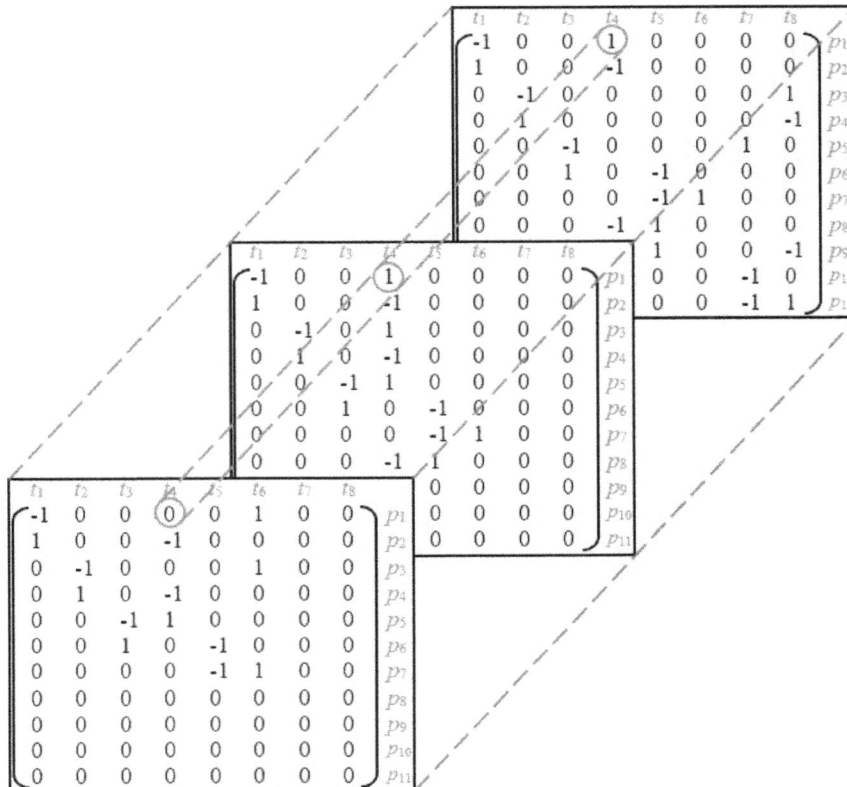

First alternative Petri net (back):

	t_1	t_2	t_3	t_4	t_5	t_6	t_7	t_8	
p_1	-1	0	0	1	0	0	0	0
p_2	1	0	0	-1	0	0	0	0
p_3	0	-1	0	0	0	0	0	1
p_4	0	1	0	0	0	0	0	-1
p_5	0	0	-1	0	0	0	1	0
p_6	0	0	1	0	-1	0	0	0
p_7	0	0	0	0	-1	1	0	0
p_8	0	0	0	-1	1	0	0	0
p_9					1	0	0	-1
p_{10}					0	0	-1	0
p_{11}					0	0	-1	1

Second alternative Petri net (middle):

	t_1	t_2	t_3	t_4	t_5	t_6	t_7	t_8	
p_1	-1	0	0	1	0	0	0	0
p_2	1	0	0	-1	0	0	0	0
p_3	0	-1	0	1	0	0	0	0
p_4	0	1	0	-1	0	0	0	0
p_5	0	0	-1	1	0	0	0	0
p_6	0	0	1	0	-1	0	0	0
p_7	0	0	0	0	-1	1	0	0
p_8	0	0	0	-1	1	0	0	0
p_9	0	0	0	0
p_{10}	0	0	0	0
p_{11}	0	0	0	0

Third alternative Petri net (front):

	t_1	t_2	t_3	t_4	t_5	t_6	t_7	t_8	
p_1	-1	0	0	0	0	1	0	0
p_2	1	0	0	-1	0	0	0	0
p_3	0	-1	0	0	0	1	0	0
p_4	0	1	0	-1	0	0	0	0
p_5	0	0	-1	1	0	0	0	0
p_6	0	0	1	0	-1	0	0	0
p_7	0	0	0	0	-1	1	0	0
p_8	0	0	0	0	0	0	0	0
p_9	0	0	0	0	0	0	0	0
p_{10}	0	0	0	0	0	0	0	0
p_{11}	0	0	0	0	0	0	0	0

Figure 4.
Overlapping the incidence matrices of the alternative Petri nets.

4.3.1.3 Step 3: comparing the elements of the incidence matrices

Before merging the alternative Petri nets into a single compound Petri net, the elements of their incidence matrices at the same position should be compared. As an outcome of this comparison, it is possible to identify which elements of the resulting compound Petri net present a specific value or its value should be chosen from a set of feasible values, leading to a structural parameter.

In general, all the numbers defining the different features of the Petri net should be compared to identify the parameters of the resulting compound Petri net.

This comparison has been depicted in **Figure 4**, where the incidence matrices of all the alternative Petri nets have been depicted. These incidence matrices are overlapped in order to ease the comparison of each element in the three matrices. Additionally, the comparison of the element was placed in the first row and fourth column. Due to the fact that the elements at this position do not present the same value in all the incidence matrices, the resulting compound Petri net would have a structural parameter in this position.

A result of the comparison of the elements of the incidence matrices can be seen in **Figure 5**. At the positions where all the values of the incidence matrices are the same, these values have been represented in the matrix of **Figure 5**. Additionally, where the values are not the same, the complete range of feasible values, depending on the incidence matrix, has been represented.

4.3.1.4 Step 4: defining the parameters of the compound Petri net

Once the comparison of the different numbers defining the Petri net has been performed, it is possible to define a parameter for each set of noncoinciding numbers. As it can be seen in **Figure 5**, there are 17 positions, where the elements of the depicted matrix do not present a single value, but a set of 3 different possibilities. As a consequence, the resulting compound Petri net would include 17 structural parameters.

As it has been mentioned in Section 2.2, rows and columns of an incidence matrix can be swapped without modifying the structure or the behavior of the net. It is possible to profit from this property trying to rearrange the elements of the incidence matrices of the alternative Petri nets in order to minimize the number of structural parameters in the resulting compound Petri net.

The incidence matrix of the resulting compound Petri net has been detailed in **Figure 6**. This incidence matrix presents the 17 structural parameters in the

	t_1	t_2	t_3	t_4	t_5	t_6	t_7	t_8	
	-1	0	0	$\{0,1,1\}$	0	$\{1,0,0\}$	0	0	p_1
	1	0	0	-1	0	0	0	0	p_2
	0	-1	0	$\{0,1,0\}$	0	$\{1,0,0\}$	0	$\{0,0,1\}$	p_3
	0	1	0	$\{-1,-1,0\}$	0	0	0	$\{0,0,-1\}$	p_4
	0	0	-1	$\{1,1,0\}$	0	0	$\{0,0,1\}$	0	p_5
	0	0	1	0	-1	0	0	0	p_6
	0	0	0	0	-1	1	0	0	p_7
	0	0	0	$\{0,-1,-1\}$	$\{0,1,1\}$	0	0	0	p_8
	0	0	0	0	$\{0,0,1\}$	0	0	$\{0,0,-1\}$	p_9
	0	0	0	$\{0,0,1\}$	0	0	$\{0,0,-1\}$	0	p_{10}
	0	0	0	0	0	0	$\{0,0,-1\}$	$\{0,0,1\}$	p_{11}

Figure 5.
Analysis of differences in the elements of the three incidence matrices.

$$W(R^c) = \begin{array}{c} \\ \\ \\ \\ \\ \\ \\ \\ \\ \\ \\ \end{array} \left(\begin{array}{cccccccc} t_1 & t_2 & t_3 & t_4 & t_5 & t_6 & t_7 & t_8 \\ -1 & 0 & 0 & \alpha_1 & 0 & \alpha_2 & 0 & 0 \\ 1 & 0 & 0 & -1 & 0 & 0 & 0 & 0 \\ 0 & -1 & 0 & \alpha_3 & 0 & \alpha_4 & 0 & \alpha_5 \\ 0 & 1 & 0 & -\alpha_6 & 0 & 0 & 0 & -\alpha_7 \\ 0 & 0 & -1 & \alpha_8 & 0 & 0 & \alpha_9 & 0 \\ 0 & 0 & 1 & 0 & -1 & 0 & 0 & 0 \\ 0 & 0 & 0 & 0 & -1 & 1 & 0 & 0 \\ 0 & 0 & 0 & -\alpha_{10} & \alpha_{11} & 0 & 0 & 0 \\ 0 & 0 & 0 & 0 & \alpha_{12} & 0 & 0 & -\alpha_{13} \\ 0 & 0 & 0 & \alpha_{14} & 0 & 0 & -\alpha_{15} & 0 \\ 0 & 0 & 0 & 0 & 0 & 0 & -\alpha_{16} & \alpha_{17} \end{array} \right) \begin{array}{c} p_1 \\ p_2 \\ p_3 \\ p_4 \\ p_5 \\ p_6 \\ p_7 \\ p_8 \\ p_9 \\ p_{10} \\ p_{11} \end{array}$$

$S_\alpha = \{\alpha_1, \alpha_2, \alpha_3, \alpha_4, \alpha_5, \alpha_6, \alpha_7, \alpha_8, \alpha_9, \alpha_{10}, \alpha_{11}, \alpha_{12}, \alpha_{13}, \alpha_{14}, \alpha_{15}, \alpha_{16}, \alpha_{17}\}$

$S_{vala} = \{(0, 1, 0, 1, 0, 1, 0, 1, 0, 0, 0, 0, 0, 0, 0, 0, 0); (1, 0, 1, 0, 0, 1, 0, 1, 0, 1, 1, 0, 0, 0, 0, 0, 0); (1, 0, 0, 0, 1, 0, 1, 0, 1, 1, 1, 1, 1, 1, 1, 1, 1)\}$

Figure 6.
Incidence matrix of the compound Petri net, set of parameters, and set of feasible combination of values for these parameters.

positions deduced in the previous step. Additionally, two sets that complete the description given by the incidence matrix are presented:

The set with the 17 parameters (all of them are structural parameters) is given under the name S_α.

The set with the feasible combinations of values for the parameters has also been presented, named S_{vala}. In this example, it is verified that $S_{valstra} = S_{vala}$. In other words, all the parameters are structural ones; hence, the set of feasible combinations of values for the structural parameters is the same as the set of feasible combinations of values for the parameters of the Petri net.

4.3.1.5 Step 5: building up the resulting compound Petri net

With the previous information, it is possible to detail all the remaining features of the resulting compound Petri net.

In **Figure 7**, the graphical representation of the compound Petri net is provided. This description should be complemented with the set of feasible combinations of values for the parameters of the Petri net, which detail the constraints applied to the parameters of the Petri nets.

4.3.2 Transformation of a compound Petri net into a set of alternative Petri nets

This transformation is quite straightforward.

Given a set $S_{valstra}$ of feasible combination of values for the structural parameters of the Petri net, let us call $q = \text{card}(S_{valstra})$, number of these combinations of values. This set can be represented as $S_{valstr} = \{cv_1, cv_2, ..., cv_q\}$.

4.3.2.1 Step 1: obtaining the first alternative Petri net

Let us consider $cv_1 \in S_{valstr}$. Let us substitute the k components of cv_1 in the k structural parameters of the compound Petri net $S_{stra} = \{\alpha_1, \alpha_2, ..., \alpha_k\}$.

The resulting Petri net from this substitution might contain nonstructural parameters but not structural ones. As a consequence, it is a component of a set of alternative Petri nets.

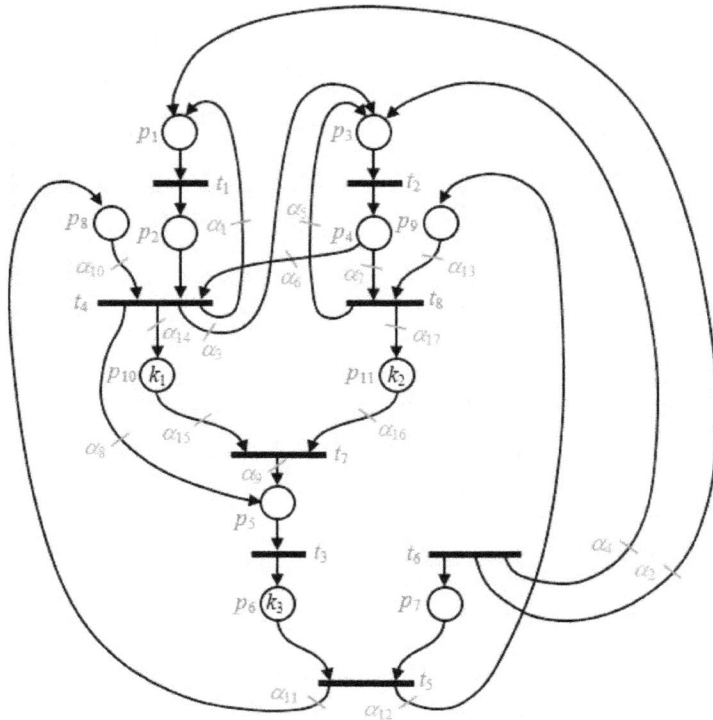

Figure 7.
Compound Petri net.

4.3.2.2 Step 2: obtaining the rest alternative Petri nets

Let us choose sequentially the elements of S_{valstr} and, for each one of them, repeat Step 1.

5. Conclusions

Simulation is a very useful tool for analyzing the structure and, specially, the behavior of the model of a discrete event system. It is a particularly interesting tool, when applied to the development of decision support systems.

However, simulation is a demanding task for a computer, requiring a certain amount of resources, such as memory and processing time.

A Petri net is a modeling formalism that has been broadly and successfully used in a large range of applications. A Petri net model of a discrete event system in a decision process may present degrees of freedom in the initial marking, the incidence matrices, or other components of the model, such as delay times or priorities.

In order to alleviate the modeling process by Petri nets of discrete event systems with degrees of freedom, as well as with the purpose of increasing the efficiency of simulation-based decision making, an analysis of two Petri net–based formalisms has been studied.

In particular, a set of alternative Petri nets and a compound Petri nets has been defined, compared, transformed one into the other, and applied to an illustrative example.

As a conclusion, both formalisms allow modeling a Petri net with alternative structural configurations and provide different characteristics that can be useful in different stages of the application of the model, for example, in the development of a decision support system.

Furthermore, the transformation of one model described using the formalism of the set of alternative Petri nets into an equivalent model represented as a compound Petri net is feasible and may be automated easily. Additionally, the inverse transformation can also be developed and it is even more straightforward than the previous one. These algorithms allow disconnecting the different stages of decision-making support, since the modeling process might be developed using a set of alternative Petri nets, if it is more intuitive, and an equivalent compound Petri net can be developed to be applied for simulation.

Compound Petri nets may produce a significant reduction in the size of the model of a discrete event system, which might alleviate significantly the computer resources required by a decision support system. This statement is based on the fact that when the different alternative structural configurations are similar, which is very common in the design of products, the size of the incidence matrix of the compound Petri net is very similar to the largest incidence matrix of the alternative Petri nets, and the amount of structural parameters may not be large.

Author details

Juan-Ignacio Latorre-Biel[1] and Emilio Jiménez-Macías[2]*

1 Institute of Smart Cities, Public University of Navarre, Pamplona, Spain

2 Department of Electrical Engineering, University of La Rioja, Logroño, Spain

*Address all correspondence to: emilio.jimenez@unirioja.es

IntechOpen

References

[1] Bruzzone AG, Longo F. An advanced system for supporting the decision process within large-scale retail stores. Simulation. 2010;**86**(12):742-762

[2] Cassandras CG, Lafortune S. Introduction to Discrete Event Systems. 2nd ed. Springer; 2008

[3] Silva M. Introducing Petri nets. In: Di Cesare F, editor. Practice of Petri Nets in Manufacturing. Chapman Hall; 1993. pp. 1-62

[4] David R, Alla H. Discrete, Continuous, and Hybrid Petri Nets. 2nd ed2010. pp. 1-550

[5] Giua A, Silva M. Petri nets and Automatic Control: A historical perspective. Annual Reviews in Control. 2018;**45**:223-239

[6] Latorre-Biel JI, Jiménez-Macías E, Blanco-Fernández J, Martínez-Cámara E, Sáenz-Díez JC, Pérez-Parte M. Decision support system, based on the paradigm of the Petri nets, for the design and operation of a dairy plant. International Journal of Food Engineering. 2015;**11**(6):767-776

[7] Piera MA, Music G. Coloured Petri net scheduling models: timed state space exploration shortages. Mathematics and Computers in Simulation. 2011;**82**(3): 428-441

[8] Latorre JI, Jiménez E, Pérez M. The optimization problem based on alternatives aggregation Petri nets as models for industrial discrete event systems. Simulation. 2013;**89**(3):346-361

[9] Zaitsev DA, Shmeleva TR. A parametric colored Petri net model of a switched network. International Journal of Communications, Network and System Sciences. 2011;**04**(01):65-76

[10] Baruwa OT, Piera MA. A coloured Petri net-based hybrid heuristic search approach to simultaneous scheduling of machines and automated guided vehicles. International Journal of Production Research. 2016;**54**(16): 4773-4792

[11] Latorre-Biel J-I, Jiménez-Macías E, Pérez-Parte M. Sequence of decisions on discrete event systems modeled by Petri nets with structural alternative configurations. Journal of Computational Science. 2014;**5**(3): 387-394

[12] Bruzzone AG, Massei M. Simulation-based military training. In: Mittal S, Durak U, Ören T, editors. Guide to Simulation-Based Disciplines. Simulation Foundations, Methods and Applications. Cham: Springer; 2017

[13] Longo F, Nicoletti L, Chiurco A, Solis A, Massei M, Diaz R. Investigating the behavior of a shop order manufacturing system by using simulation. In: Proceedings of the Emerging M and S Applications in Industry and Academia Symposium, EAIA 2013 and the Modeling and Humanities Symposium 2013, MatH 2013, Part of the 2013 Spring Simulation Multiconference, SpringSim 2013, USA. April 2013. pp. 47-54

[14] Mota MM, Piera MA. A compact timed state space approach for the analysis of manufacturing systems: Key algorithmic improvements. International Journal of Computer Integrated Manufacturing. 2011;**24**(2): 135-153

[15] Latorre-Biel JI, Jiménez E, Pérez M, Leiva F, Martínez E, Blanco J. Simulation model of a production facility of *Agaricus bisporus* mycelium for decision-making support. International Journal of Food

Engineering. 2017;**14**(2):1-16. Article ID
20170159. DOI: 10.1515/ijfe-2017-0159

[16] Latorre-Biel JI, Jimenez-Macias E,
Perez-Parte M, Blanco-Fernandez J,
Martinez-Camara E. Control of discrete
event systems by means of discrete
optimization and disjunctive colored
PNs: Application to manufacturing
facilities. Abstract and Applied Analysis.
2014:1-16. Article ID 821707. DOI:
10.1155/2014/821707

[17] Latorre-Biel J-I, Jiménez-Macías E,
Blanco-Fernández J, Sáenz-Díez JC.
Optimal design of an olive oil mill by
means of the simulation of a Petri net
model. International Journal of Food
Engineering. 2014;**10**(4):573-582

[18] Recalde L, Silva M, Ezpeleta J,
Teruel E. Petri Nets and Manufacturing
Systems: An Examples-Driven Tour. In:
Lectures on Concurrency and Petri
Nets, vol. 3098 of Lecture Notes in
Computer Science. Berlin, Heidelberg:
Springer; 2004. pp. 742-788

[19] Tsinarakis GJ, Tsourveloudis NC,
Valavanis KP. Petri net modeling of
routing and operation flexibility in
production systems. In: Proceedings of
the 20th IEEE International Symposium
on Intelligent Control, ISIC'05 and the
13th Mediterranean Conference on
Control and Automation, MED'05.
Cyprus; June 2005. pp. 352-357

[20] Latorre-Biel J-I, Jiménez-Macías E,
Pérez-De-La-Parte M, Sáenz-Díez JC,
Martínez-Cámara E, Blanco-Fernández J.
Compound Petri nets and alternatives
aggregation Petri nets: Two formalisms
for decision-making support.
Advances in Mechanical Engineering.
2016;**8**(11):1-12

[21] Latorre-Biel JI, Jiménez-Macías E,
Pérez De La Parte M. Equivalent and
efficient optimization models for an
industrial discrete event system with
alternative structural configurations.

Complexity. **2018**:14. Article ID
5341346. DOI: 10.1155/2018/5341346

www.ingramcontent.com/pod-product-compliance
Lightning Source LLC
Chambersburg PA
CBHW081243190326
41458CB00016B/5892